A German Tale

A GERMAN TALE

A Girl Surviving Hitler's Legacy

ERIKA V. SHEARIN KARRES

BARRICADE
BOOKS

Fort Lee, New Jersey

Published by Barricade Books Inc.
185 Bridge Plaza North
Suite 308-A
Ft. Lee, NJ 07024

Library of Congress Cataloging-in-Publication Data
Pending at the time of publication.
Contact the Library of Congress for this information.

First Printing

CONTENTS

DEDICATION

Long is the way
And hard, that out of hell leads up to light.
—John Milton,
Paradise Lost

❦ ❦ ❦

This book is written in memory of my mother, Barbara Schmelzer Vierling, who died at 41, Julie Dommes Vierling, my stepmother, who died at 45, and Heda Vierling Kochta, my oldest sister, who was killed at 34.

—

And with love for my daughters, Elizabeth Shearin Hounshell and Dr. Mary D. Shearin, and my husband, Andrew Matthew Karres.

—

And with gratitude for June Clark, my agent, who encouraged me to look at my early years through the kaleidoscope of time and let the memories come.

—

And for Allan J. Wilson, my editor at Barricade Books, whose powerful vision, expertise and brilliance brought those memories to life.

—

And for *Vati.*

"...At 13, I shoot up several centimeters and leave my two older sisters behind.

When I corner my father one day, I can now look him straight in the eyes. They are light gray like those rocks on top of the Alps that have been exposed to the elements for thousands of years.

What happened with the Jews? I ask.

He's not able to meet my eyes. I don't know.

I stand there facing him, arms folded. I notice I'm holding my breath.

It was like this, he says, looking over my shoulder. Once I wanted to see what all that big to-do was about. So I went to a Nazi rally. It was held inside that beautiful auditorium. Do you remember it? Of course, it was bombed out, but it was the one built in the early style of—

I cut him off. And? My voice is hard. So what? I don't care about the auditorium.

—A party boss was speaking. What a clown, let me tell you. Short guy, beer belly, greasy lederhosen, suspenders, knee socks, tassels. The works. Whenever he finished a sentence, everybody jumped up. Everybody. They raised their arms in a Nazi salute and screamed Heil Hitler. That noise and all those idiots. He's looking at me now. Ach Gott, *it was disgusting.*

What did you do?

I didn't jump up or salute. That's for sure. What do you think I am?... A pause.... So these young thugs start beating me over the head every time I don't jump up. They rolled up a stack of programs and let me have it. Whack-whack. On top of my head every time. Believe me, I got out of there just as fast as I could.

I let my breath out. That's what I've been waiting for all my life, answers. The truth.

9

Another deep breath: And then?

Then nothing.

My heart plummets. That's it?...You walked out of some damn Nazi rally?

No, of course not. There was a wonderful Jewish-owned store in town....The owner and I were the best of friends. Like brothers really. We could talk about every-thing. Philosophy, politics, religion. So of course I kept going there. To pick up a few items, play some chess. You know, it was like a regular corner store where you drop in. Stay as long as you like. One day I open the newspaper and see pictures of some of the people who went there with the caption: Enemies of the People. Mensch, *did I get furious. Enraged—that's how I felt. Violated. Those Nazi assholes, how dare they!*

And then what? I say feeling better again.

Then nothing. I stopped going there. What good would it have done having my picture in the paper? Hmm? His hand lands on my shoulder. He's shaking me, trying to make me understand. Don't forget, I had a wife and kids to think about. Naturally first I checked on those poor people already branded Enemy of the People. Know what happened to them?　　　˙

No.

They were hauled off in the middle of the night and never heard from again.

I shrug his hand off. Then what did you do? I notice I'm holding my breath again.

A sigh. You know, I was always apolitical.

Is that the same as amoral?

He looks at me hard. Hauls back and slaps me across the face...."

FOREWORD

White Rose

In the early 1940s, while the world first watched and finally the allied victory stops the Holocaust, not everyone inside the Third Reich cows down to the madness engulfing Germany. One example: One day in 1942 during the height of the Nazi regime, a small group of college students meets at the University of Munich to start a resistance movement, called *Weisse Rose* (White Rose).

It's a clandestine meeting headed up by a brother and sister. Hans Scholl, the brother, had been an orderly on the Eastern Front where he saw the atrocities committed against the Jews. His sister Sophie watched the Jews in Bavaria rounded up and is outraged.

At the meeting a young German soldier tells about the Action Groups. Those are *SS Einsatz Gruppen*—units of 800 to 3,000 men that follow the German Army as it marches against the Soviet Union.

They're usually headed up by professional men and include ministers, scientists, physicians, artists, lawyers....Many are intellectuals in their early 30s and use their brain power to become "efficient executioners."

Later one Action Group leader said that victims were rounded up and trucked to the execution sites, which were anti-tank ditches. "Then they were shot, kneeling or standing, by firing squads....The corpses were thrown into the ditch." Another witness tells of seeing heaps of shoes, 800 to 1,000 pairs, and piles of underwear and clothes at a mass grave in the Ukraine. "The pit," he says, "was already two-thirds full and contained about 1,000 people."

❦ ❦ ❦

Of course, the secret student meeting is reported to the Nazis, and the participants are executed. More than 100 other people are also arrested. While their fate is never publicized, everyone knows what it was. And from then on, people who are too scared to speak out openly for fear that they and their families will face a similar fate start planting white rose bushes.

Or wish they could.

❦ ❦ ❦

One such person is a slightly overweight young woman living in the northeastern part of Germany, Barbara Schmelzer. At 5'2" with shimmering black hair, sparkling green eyes and porcelain skin, she is so pretty that as a teenager, she wins a beauty contest at a country fair. The extra weight doesn't pile on until she has kids.

She comes from a modest background. Like millions of Germans, she first admires everything the Nazi regime stands for. She's proud to be German, proud of Adolf Hitler because she believes he'll get her country out from under the yoke of World War I reparations, plus make it flourish again. Not that she's ever seen any of it. She never goes anywhere, but the big promises and fiery speeches sound good to her. Every time she hears Hitler speak, it's like a sip of champagne.

Fact is, during most of the 1930s she's just happy. Even though she has only an elementary education and is in training to become a children's practical nurse, she's met one of the most dashing bachelors of Bavaria. And, miracle of miracles, he's fallen in love with her. Her Hans also studied at the University of Munich, but he already received his doctoral degree in electrical engineering in 1933. Plus, he's from the oldest family in Weiden, a historic city in the Palatinate, where his family's been known since the Middle Ages and prominent since the 1500s.

What good fortune. Hans's father is a highly respected physician with a bristling white mustache and penetrating dark eyes who took care of Bavarian royalty before the first World War. His mother's a fine lady, speaks English and French fluently, and used to march for the women's right to vote. So of course Barbara's happy. That's some jump up in society, *nicht wahr?* Never mind that Hans's family plumb hates her. Even her own family goes: Tsk-tsk-tsk. Don't you remember that old fairy tale? About that prince marrying a pretty commoner? When the girl went swimming one day, the King sent divers out to drag her underwater. Drowned her good....

Pah. Barbara smiles. Won't happen to me. I'm too good a swimmer. Anyway, it's nothing but pure jealousy behind those frowns, icy stares, all that tsk-tsk-tsking. She goes right ahead and marries Dr. Hans Vierling, the eldest son of Dr. Gustav Vierling, who's also the son of a doctor. And so on and so forth way back into history....

Barbara beams and beams: I did it. And isn't her husband incredible? Such a handsome man and a genius to boot. And she's no slouch either. Hitler's emphasis on women having as many kids as possible suits her fine. She throws herself into being the perfect housewife and *Mutter*, pops out seven kids in six years: first a girl, then a boy. Then two sets of twins! Then another girl.

The first three are beautiful, healthy babies. Too bad the last four die, but that's all right too. Obviously not good specimens, what with that food rationing soon to come and the war making life so *verdammt* difficult.

It's not quite that simple: One of the last four sick babies survived. Pitiful little thing, a cripple really. Barbara should've taken the doctor's advice when he said: Don't feel bad. Just a biological error. Let's pitch it out and forget about it.

No! For some reason Barbara shook her head. Now she wonders why. Daily that little girl's turning into a bigger burden. She's suffering from rickets, which makes her legs curve outward like bent switches. When she starts crawling, she scoots around on the insides of her ankles. A bird with broken wings looks better. One good thing—she knows she's a disappointment....Most of the time she hides in a corner ashamed, bangs her head against the wall, a stony expression on her face.

Won't last long, poor little thing. Thank *Gott*!

But the older children are such a joy. So smart, strong, pretty. They'll live in the best world possible when they get grown. It's up to Barbara to ensure they make it.

How she dives into her *Hausfrau* duties, bakes *Plaetzchen*, cooks *Eintopf* stews, sews *Kleider* and *Hoeschen*, scrubs and waxes the *Diele* so hard that she can see her big smile reflect in the hardwood floor, then does it all over again. But an uneasiness settles on her like a cement blanket and won't go away. Each time she steps outside, there's all kinds of nice folks being rounded up. Herds of human sheep. Plus, she hears about former neighbors suddenly being shipped off to strange places. Odd. On top of that, all those rumors: Those poor people won't ever come back....

All lies, sure. Still, makes you wonder, doesn't it? Her own *Familienbuch* is perfect, thank *Gott*! And Hans's family records date back further than anyone else's in town. But once he told her in a hushed voice, "Two Jews married into my family years ago. They turned Catholics, but don't ever tell." Which of course, she wouldn't. What does he think she is—*dumm*?

Yet from then on, whenever Barbara notices any sign of the Storm Troopers, she darts into a side street. One day she sees a hard-faced soldier knock a bearded old man to the ground and runs to help the old man up. Brush him off. The soldier grabs her arm hard, raises his hand to slap her, notices her stomach that looks like risen dough. With a curse he lets her go. She is fuming: Nothing like that would've happened just a year or two ago. What's going on?

From then on, no matter how hard she tries not to see upsetting things, she sees everything. How groceries are shut and boarded up. Furniture is flung on the streets for passers-by to pick at like pigeons do bread crumbs. When no soldiers are around, people cry openly. You can smell their fear in the air. It's scary. All kinds of worries attack her like a mosquito swarm. Now people talk only in whispers and everything's forbidden. You can't read foreign newspapers anymore, listen to the radio stations you want. Her car is confiscated, then the hunting guns. Every place you look is crawling with uniforms. Then it's curfews. Food rations. Having to drape blankets over the windows at night. So enemy planes won't target your house, drop bombs.

Bombs, bombs, bombs.

But what about the enemies in town? All those young thugs in uniform? Nobody stops them. *Ach*, life's so hard now.

Then the worst: Suddenly Barbara can't go to mass anymore. The church is bolted; smashed stained-glass windows are red, blue, green and yellow teardrops on the sidewalk. The priest is hauled off. Why? And why now when her little cripple's still a heathen? If she could only get the child christened before she dies.

And if she could only ask her Hans about what's going on. He's so smart; he'd explain things. Barbara aches not being able to see his handsome face with the startling light-gray eyes, noble bone structure, narrow red lips, perfect white teeth....Oh, his well-shaped head with the precise haircut. She'd give anything to touch his athletic body, hold his beautiful hands, listen to his resonant voice. Whenever she's sick, he talks to her like a child, always knows just what to give her to make her better. Helps her with the circular hair loss she's developed. Drops, pills—he can get anything. After all, medicine is in his blood.

But he's been drafted. Before the war started, he got offers every day to join the Party, move up the ranks, be a Nazi leader. But he turned them all down. Too busy. Have to work on my inventions....

Once the war started, three men in uniform knocked on the door one day and escorted him to the induction center. Ever since, he's been working for the war effort. The few times he comes home, his lips are pale; his face, ashen. In the middle of the day, he lies on the sofa, on a striped lawn chair in the yard. Haven't slept in ages, he says. Those assholes broke my spine. His voice is lifeless.

And yet Barbara smells the scent of another woman on him. *Ach! Ach!*

Then good news. Finally. A neighbor comes running: Barbara, have you heard about the brand-new children's bunker?

No, where?

In downtown Magdeburg. That's a big city close by. All sorts of delicious food and fine feather bedding are being stockpiled in that new bunker. It's for women and kids only.

The neighbor explains that the war's going bad right now. That's obvious. So the plan is to round up Germany's future generation. Make sure they're safe from enemy bombs.

Relieved, Barbara spends the next few days sorting through the kids' outfits. She packs a suitcase for the children. In her own she tucks jewelry, the pink and baby-blue Meissen figurines, pieces of her best Dresden china, ornate silverware, small oil paintings, Hans's rare books bound in leather, her furs, photos. Whatever she can cram in.

The suitcases weigh a ton. She can barely drag them, especially with that little worm suddenly clinging to her. The older children see her packing: Where're we going, *Mutti*?

Into town.

Where in town?

To a wonderful underground camp.

Ooh, oh, tralala. The children sing and clap their hands. We're going on vacation. Barbara is excited too. The bombing now comes almost daily. Just got to get away from here, where the worst battles are. As far away from the war as I can. Save the children....

Fortunately already, black touring cars snake into the neighborhood. Look, down the street, soldiers stride from door to door. They round up all mothers and children.

What a relief. Now Barbara won't have to worry about getting food anymore. No more being scared the house is bombed. The older kids are dancing around her, three golden heirs of the *Reich*—all smart, pretty, healthy. The little cripple sags in a corner—a bag of laundry, but always watching, always listening. A hurt little animal, a lynx lying in wait.

Odd, that one is.

As the round-up cars get closer, Barbara feels the hair in back of her neck rise. Suddenly she has a vision of bunkers filled with women and kids—and they're screaming. *Screaming.* Her heart starts beating fast. She scrambles around for a map. Isn't there anyplace in the world that's not engulfed by war?

Only America. But that's across the ocean. She remembers grainy old newsreels showing a stately lady from the U.S., Mrs. Eleanor Roosevelt. No beauty, but kind looking, like somebody you could entrust your children to….

The Nazi limousines are three houses away. How efficient those stone-faced soldiers are. How they gather and shoo all females and their offspring. Barbara sighs. *Lieber Gott*, oh why is America so far? But then she remembers hearing that the southern part of Germany hasn't been hit too bad and claps her hands: *Kinder*, c'mon, *schnell*, let's go. She rushes them down the hall.

No, Mama. No. We want to ride in the big cars.

Later. First let's go on a picnic.

They're out the back door just as a car pulls up in front. Hurry, hurry! Barbara's dragging the suitcases, the little cripple clinging to her back like a rucksack. When her doorbell rings, she and the kids are running down a lane, into the thick woods. Barbara looks back. Oh, her pretty new house…. All her fine furniture….

Damn that old war. But it can't last much longer now, can it? Soon Hans has to come home from the front. She's circled a place on the map for him, so he'll find her. Then she'll make *verdammt!* sure he'll forget all about that hussy. She's heard of those loose women who follow the soldiers everywhere.

On the outskirts of town, they pass an old chapel. A priest, twisted by age, is ducking out of sight. Wait, she begs. She just remembered that she's forgotten to pack food. The older kids can make it without supper. And in the morning some farmer will feed them. Sure. But the little one's so spindly already, she won't last. Could you christen this child, please?

The priest peeks around. What name? Quick.

Eleanor.

That's it?

No. Remember when the war started? The song all those boys with their apple cheeks and shiny eyes sang?...Barbara feels tears running down her face.... Before they all got so mean? Seems like that was centuries ago, when the world was still whole. Not smashed to smithereens by all those enemy bombs. Back before people got so evil. Don't you remember? *Auf der Heide steht ein kleines Bluemelein und*—(On the heather grows a little floweret, and—).

The priest's bones creak. He straightens and spits. Sure, I remember. He picks up where she left off and finishes the song—*das heisst* (it's called)—*Erika*. But don't pick that name, please. No. His voice quivers. That's the march our boys sang on their way to hell.

CHAPTER 1

Death Crawl

I was born in Magdeburg, a city near Berlin, two weeks after Germany marched on Poland. My earliest memories are of violence. Bombs. Loud noises, sounds of explosions. Shrieks, screams. I had no toys. No childhood. Never played, never laughed. Death and destruction were everyday events. Amazing I lived through that time, and wouldn't have if my mother hadn't been so courageous. If she'd stayed put in the Northeast, one of two things would have happened:

If I'd been lucky, I would have grown up in Communist East Germany.

And if I hadn't been lucky?

I'll get to that.

But first, how did Barbara carry me and two big suitcases, and walk with her three other small kids all across the hundreds of miles from the Northeast of Germany to the Southwest?

To Bavaria?

Nobody helped her and her legs ached constantly. Ever since the last baby died, her legs were swollen. They hurt, especially her calves. Her veins were inflamed. I don't remember much of the long trek, except for the many times when low-flying planes strafed us. We had to run for our lives. Run, run, run. Fling ourselves into a ditch to keep from getting hit. Head down, freeze, pray.

Pop-pop-pop. The ammunition always hit the ground all around us, making the brown earth spit. Vomit up dirt clumps that rained on us. We got scratches, nervous tics.

My mother always throws herself on top of us. Her scratches are big. They fester. My legs, oh my legs, she says. She wears rubber stockings that don't help. The doctor has told her: Rest, take it easy, no lifting, prop up your feet, take a nap, eat good food. Otherwise there's the danger of a blood clot....

She does the opposite: runs, rushes, hurries as quickly as she can away from Magdeburg. Four small kids cling to her as she drags the bulging suitcases. But she's determined to get us to a safe place. First west, then south. And every step she hurts. I remember her beautiful face twisted in pain. Sweat beads roll down her forehead as she bends and massages her calves, yet never lets go of me. She can't. I cling to her, a big blob of marmalade.

By the time Barbara reaches Bavaria, her legs are as big as tree trunks. Yet she keeps going, settles us into an old house in Diessen am Ammersee, not far from the Alps. The house has a red, steeply pitched roof with large sections missing, torn stucco walls, and desperately clings to a hill. It belongs to Hans's mother, now a widow, a stern lady always swathed in black silk dotted with antique pins. Silver that looks like pewter. She never approved of Barbara, and the house acts the same way. It hates us: There's no power, the kitchen is bare. Chunks of walls have smashed the furniture. It's winter, a typical Bavarian winter—ice cold. Military-gray skies dump snow every day. Only with coaxing does water trickle from the freezing pipes. How they clang. The hungry kids scream, their faces blue.

Barbara dresses them in all their clothes. Layers of shirts, pants, jackets. Wool hats, scarves, mittens. Still they shiver inside the cold house as they huddle on her bed with blankets piled on top. In the dark, the baby is a block of ice.

Barbara spends all her days trying to get the kids warm. She forces herself out into the snow. With the last of her strength chops down a tree, which takes hours. The axe is dull. She crawls back in the house, hauling snow-covered branches behind her. Her crawling starts out slow and gets slower, like the time passing in the icy ruin of a house. Hours later Barbara drags a frozen branch inside, thaws it out in the bed, makes a fire around which they huddle. She can't ever go to sleep. The fire has to be stoked constantly. Icicles growing on the ceiling have to be knocked off. The floor is too cold for the kids to walk on, so she carries them to the bucket. Why do *Pisse* and *Scheisse* still stink when they're frozen?

The kids cry, all except the baby whose face gets

bluer, thinner, stonier. They only doze off when Barbara reads to them from a forbidden leaflet. Or tells them about their long march. How far they walked step for step, how they dragged along with those lead suitcases. How brave they were. Don't you remember? I didn't know which way to turn, where west was. Or south. But there was always a light in the sky....

Oh Mama. The kids know what that was—just more war stuff, artillery, explosions, planes shooting other planes. Boom-boom-boom. Fortunately their house hasn't been hit directly like the others in the small town. The injured stone walls are thick. The roof gapes. Snow falls into the attic but not down to the ground floor. But the best thing: The yard's over-grown with giant bushes. Firs, beeches, linden trees and oaks also shield it from view. So the enemy planes don't know there's a house.

From a window in the attic you see a glow far in the distance—Munich burning. Yet out here in the country you only see the bombs flying overhead in the sky. Then the air shifts, contracts, gets heavy. The bombs smack down somewhere but always miss the house.

So far.

Burrowed deep in their ice house, Barbara blows on the kids' frozen hands and faces for warmth. She rubs their feet. All the kids have frostbite. The blue skin on their toes splits like sausage boiled too long and curls back, revealing what looks like peeled plums. But heating water and dipping in the frozen toes help. It still hurts but eventually the little toes start to heal. By then Barbara can hardly move herself. Her huge legs are raw, but she inches herself up once a day, scrounges up wormy oatmeal. Some barley to make watery soup, thin gray broth.

It's so good.

On days when the snow stops, Barbara hobbles to the Diessen town square to see if she can "buy" some food on the black market. All the china, jewelry and artworks she's lugged those hundreds of miles come in handy. Once when she gets to the square, she hears women screaming. What's the matter?

Last night....Didn't you hear?

No, what? What?

Another terrible bombing in the Northeast. A huge air raid. Hundreds of thousands wiped out—

Barbara feels faint and clutches her heart. No, don't tell me. Not my Hans, please. Please. Please! She fears the Fliegerhorst (Air Force Station) Koethen where her husband is stationed has been hit. Where was it? Where?

It wasn't Koethen.

Thank God. From relief Barbara crumples on the street.

It was Magdeburg. The whole city's been flattened. Wiped out.

Oh, no, no, no. All those poor moms and kids in the bunkers! And her house, her neighbors, her husband's company, the big beautiful churches, the majestic bridges over the Elbe River—gone.

All gone.

Gone with the war.

❦ ❦ ❦

Fact: By fall 1944, Germany has lost the war. Hitler's Third Reich is just an ugly monster in the last throes of death. Yet on January 16, 1945, a huge contingent of Royal Air Force planes leaves England and heads toward Eastern Germany. By then every German city with more than 100,000 people has been given a code name. Magdeburg is "Young Salmon." The RAF's dinner for that evening will be smoked young salmon.

At the same time, several squadrons of American bombers head out from France for the same destination. First they destroy the city's warning system. It's late: People are already in bed. Only when the first signal bombs, called "Christmas Trees," start lighting up every street bright as a noon sun, do the shocked people scramble for shelter. Very few make it. For the next 38 minutes, the city is attacked nonstop. According to some historians, it's the most deadly 38 minutes in all of World War II.

Firebombs rain from the sky in carpet-fashion. Section after section of the city ignites. A huge fireball can be seen 50 miles away. That fireball creates such enormous winds that thousands of people are sucked out of their homes and burn to death. Whoosh. Those who manage to run to the bunkers are overcome by poison fumes.

The same happens to the thousands of mothers and children already in the bunkers. The poison gas seeps in, but when the panicked mothers claw holes in the walls and push their children out on the streets, the children come back screaming. The pavement has melted. So they burn or suffocate, including all those kids collected from the surrounding areas and brought into town for special safekeeping.

When the bombing stops, the population of 360,000 is reduced to less than 90,000. Three out of every four people are dead. The rest are alive but dead inside.

Later the charred remains of tens of thousands are scraped into buckets and dumped into a huge pit that is dug near the train station. Over and over the same unusual configurations of burned bones are discovered: charred female skeletons fused together with a small one. Or several small ones. A dying mother trying desperately to protect her kids from harm.

Only Dresden and Cologne suffer more destruction than Magdeburg. My mother, like a salmon knowing when it's time to swim upstream, sensed death hovering over that city. That's why she escaped. And I grow up knowing she saved me from burning to death.

But for what? To starve and freeze to death in Bavaria?

And to carry the burden of shame once I know what happened in Dachau?

Is guilt to be my legacy?

🐛 🐛 🐛

Barbara is ecstatic over having saved her kids. Then more good news: All soldiers are now being released from the front or are running away. So with her last ounce of strength, she crawls around the house. Dusts, sweeps, polishes the ice house. Trades her wedding band for a cup of flour, which she saves, and on swollen knees scrubs the dirty front steps.

Spring comes, ice melts, the earth softens: time to plant white roses. Miraculously, the kids still have all their toes and fingers. And even the cripple starts pulling herself up, takes a step. Life's getting better every day, *jajaja*. Just got to keep going till my handsome Hans gets home. He'll take over when he gets here. Sure he will.

Barbara works day and night, tears rags into strips to hook colorful rugs. Crochets doilies, knits sweaters, digs in the yard. Never mind her joints ache, her ankles are balloons. Her calves hurt like knives sticking in them when she walks. Must keep going until Hans—!

One day she looks over the fence. A thin old man is tottering up the hill. But he's not on crutches and not blind. His wounds are all on the inside. She can't see them and even if she could, doesn't care. Hans, oh Hans.

Kinder, come here. It's your *Vati*. Quickly she whips the little bit of precious flour into dough. Must bake a cake....

I see a young man with an old face, premature gray hair, light eyes that have seen so much that the color has leached out. A face that looks chiseled out of rare pale wood. He is silent for stretches, then words burst from him in gales. He laughs overbright: You know what my friends, the Russian prisoners, told me? I always looked after them, tossed my allotment of cigarettes into the chicken-wire cage where they were kept. Brought them apples when nobody was looking. Well, they said, when Russia wins the war, they'll pay me back for all my kindness and just plain shoot me. All the other Germans they'll get their hands on, they will gouge out their eyes, tear them limb from—

Hans, please. Don't scare the children.

But Mutti is happy. Now everything's fine. She can finally put her feet up. They can go forward again. They all made it, even the sickly little one. Surely love will erase all the horrible memories, hardships, nightmares. The roses will bloom; they'll go swimming at the lake....

That night she wakes up with a strong urge to cough. Not wanting to wake Hans and the kids, she tiptoes to the bathroom. Coughs and coughs. Stands by the window and looks at the black sky. Finally no more bombs, thank heavens. But far in the distance she sees a light again. A shooting star? Must remember to tell the children. Oh, yes, the light's moving, pointing.

Pointing to America.

Oh, how I wish! Even though the war's over, Barbara feels angry, betrayed. Her country let her down. It went bad like a rotten potato. It stinks. So many innocent people suffered, so many lives lost. Why? Why? She can't ever be proud of being German again.

Another coughing fit, this time worse. She's trying to bring up what obstructs her breathing but no use. Some of the blood clots that have lain hidden like land mines in the inflamed veins of her legs have finally worked themselves to her lungs, her heart, her brain, causing death and destruction there.

I was six.

CHAPTER 2

Salami on Dead

All mortuaries that haven't been blown up are overflowing with bodies and various human parts that nobody's been able to identify. So Mutti has no place to go. That's good, for I know she's only sleeping. Anybody can see it. Doesn't her pretty face look so peaceful, like she's finally getting a good night's rest? After all that hard work and crawling.

I stay by Mutti's side all morning and can't understand why my sister Ger, one year older, is screaming so in the yard. And why is Hansi, three years older, stomping around outside like he's killing ants? Heda, the oldest, is 11. Her face is gray and looks like Vati's, just bones now, straining to burst through her skin.

Why's everybody acting crazy? I wonder.

Sure, we can't go to school today, that's a shame. I like school, all those neat rows of kids packed on homemade wooden benches. One wrong move and you pick up splinters on your fanny, so sit still. Tall white and black figures skate between the rows. They walk, of course, those nuns, but their skirts are so long you can't see their shoes and they move gracefully, as if they were skating on the kidney-shaped Ammersee. The lake hardly ever freezes over all the way, but the end closest to Diessen is often frozen over solid. That's where we kids go skating. We have rusty skates we force onto the soles of our shoes and screw on with a key. Our worn-out soles flap loose. First we have to tie them to the tops of our shoes with a piece of string. Then on with the rusty skates.

Not now. Now we have to stay put in the yard—but not me. I'm in the house wondering: Why won't my sisters and brother stop screaming? They scream so loud it hurts my ears. And Vati acts strange too. He's stormed into the room where *Oma* (Grandmother) stays when she comes to visit, which is hardly ever.

Oma's elegant and ancient, always wears black with white lace at her throat. The lace looks like wilted petals. Her face is a shriveled flower from many years past. She's a widow; we don't know her. She didn't like Mutti marrying Vati. Doesn't like the fact that so many kids have come so fast. It's not done in her *society*.

And surely she doesn't like me. I'm partially crippled, though I can run now. Haven't I practiced?

Sure have. But maybe she'll like me better when I'll be first to report Mutti's woken up. Then Oma won't have to leave her society, come visit and comb our hair trying to rake the lice out, like she did last time. Mutti always stops when the nits won't budge and we start crying. But Oma keeps on scraping our heads with fine metal combs until she loosens the last louse egg, picks it out of our mops. The metal comb drips blood. Why's she so mean? And what's the use? The lice like us. They're our pets. Always come back in droves.

I hope Oma won't come any time soon, and where would she stay if she did? Vati's locked himself in Oma's room ever since he found out Mutti won't get up. Now Vati's in the only room in the house that's still pretty, and he is laughing his head off. It's a spine-chilling laughter that comes from deep inside him, goes on and on. It sounds like his bones are cracking. He isn't laughing. He's crying, loud as Ger.

I cower on the cold floor outside Oma's room and listen to him. Shhh, not so loud, I say but softly. Don't wake up Mutti, please!

Though she's not in bed anymore. Big crows have fluttered into the house, thin old village women from whom black rags hang. They have no faces, only points and hollows overhung by the eaves of their black kerchiefs. They sing songs with repetitious words. Melodies wail through the cold stone house, not bringing any warmth. But in contrast to Ger's screaming and Vati's cracking sounds, the wailings go up and down. So sad, so sad, the Prince married a commoner, Bavaria's ruined. Barbara's gone.

No, no, I say, Barbara's right here.

The women take over the whole house. Moving crow shadows bend over Mutti and rustle a gown that doesn't fit her. When they slice it open in the back, Mutti looks very nice in it.

They dress her for a party, roll stockings up her legs, have to stop below the massive knees. Screw her feet into her best slippers, those from before the war, with the high heels. I watch. I'm not goofing off like my sisters and my brother. Not me. I'm not locking myself in a room to make cracking sounds as if my ribs were kindling.

No. I keep my eyes on what's going on. Soon Mutti will wake up. Won't she be happy with her new hair-do, the crown the crows have woven on her head? Braids of gray hair swirled with white coil around my mother's beautiful face.

The crows pick her up. Hey, careful, don't wake her up. They pay no attention to me, hoist her downstairs into the hall outside the kitchen. The hallway is dim. What's this new strange thing? It's a sawhorse looking like a rocking horse. I climb on, but the crows push me aside, bring in a large wooden cradle, lay Mutti in it. Oh, she never looked prettier.

I'm so proud: That's my Mama.

The crows twist flowers around the cradle until they whirl like eddies. So many white, pink, dark-red and purple flowers flow around the big cradle. It's a lake of blooms. Some are goblets, some snowballs, some cabbage heads. I'm hungry, cram some petals in my mouth, but they don't taste good. The brighter the colors, the more tasteless they are.

Those blooms are just jealous of Mama because she outshines them. So they suck the color from her, make her look blue like old ice. I hate the flowers, hate their heavy smell that turns into a rotten sweet-onion stink, fills the house, seeps into me so I can't get away from it ever. Just wait until the crows scram. I'll pitch out those flowers.

But the crows settle in. Go on with their party decorations. I crawl under the sawhorse waiting. Sooner or later they'll have to skat. But when one swarm departs, another bustles through the front door. The wailing never ends, only the wailers change.

There's food in the kitchen, real food. First time in ages. Some people in town send bread, others soup. Some society folks, actual cakes. But everything tastes like the cloying flowers. I'm not hungry anyway. But just wait until Mutti wakes up. She'll kick everyone out, open windows, get that sweet-rotten smell out....

I doze under the sawhorse on Mutti's old nightie, off and on. I can never let myself drift into deep sleep. That's when she might wake up, need me to hold her hand, so she can rise from the box, swim out of the flower lake. Celebrate. The war's over.

In the morning the hall lights up, and Mutti looks even prettier. She's had a good night and smiles. Her face has color from the rays of sun slanting in. Take that, you dumb flowers!

Mutti's skin glows, ice sparkling in a cold light. Her perfect hair, not one strand out of order, shimmers. I kiss her good morning. Her cheek is harder than rock. Her arms, frozen marble columns.

Throughout the day, the flowers stink more. Mutti doesn't mind, keeps smiling. I never leave her side, don't eat anything because she doesn't. Anyway, Hansi has gotten into the cakes already.

The third day brings a new smell. It's not the flowers; it's Mutti. The sickly sweet odor has seeped into her too. I bend over her to kiss her and can't find it anymore—her lovely smell. Always since I can remember I've relied on it—the smell of my Mama filling my nostrils before falling asleep at night. Filling my tummy during the day when I'm hungry. It makes me walk on my crippled legs. Makes me push myself. Makes me run, skate, no matter how wobbly. When I fall and hurt myself, all I have to do is run to my Mama and sniff her.

Ah, all better!

Closing my eyes, burying my face in the softness that was everywhere on her, sucking up the scent of my Mama always kept me going. Stopped my pain, my tears.

Mama's scent is gone. Her softness is gone.

All gone.

I slump in a corner away from sunlight, make myself small, freeze. Hours pass, days. It's been three days since Mutti hasn't woken up. Too long.

Then a new sound besides the ones Heda, Hansi and Ger make when they clatter into the kitchen, snatch some *butterbrot*, race outside again to scream and stomp. And besides Vati's horrible cracking sounds. Strange old men lumber in, big and rough-sounding, and clamp a lid on Mutti's cradle.

But she can't breathe, I shout. No words come out. The men hoist up the box, carry it outside to an ancient vehicle, whose appearance stirs me. I move.

It's the fall of 1945, a few months after Hitler's suicide, after the end of World War II. All of Germany lies in ruins. There are no cars, no other means of transportation anywhere. But this one old truck survived. It's the first civilian vehicle in town in years. Throngs of people have been waiting for it—to leave Diessen, go back home from wherever they came, check on their bombed-out homes, see their relatives. Reunite with husbands, wives, children....

Crammed full of strange people all urgently hoping to get to their destinations as soon as possible, the truck is crawling up the hill past our house, when Vati gets it to stop. Somehow. Can't imagine what he used to bribe the driver.

I gape at the truck. In the back, hollow-eyed men and women hunker in two rows on stacks of firewood, with which the motor is stoked. There's no gasoline, so wood smoke curls from a big metal pipe sticking out of the cab.

While I'm still looking, the men sandwich Mutti's box between all the people who groan when they see Vati and us four kids. Oh no, not more folks. Under grumblings we're finally allowed to squeeze in, not that I want to. I've got to be here when Mutti wakes up. But she's in the box, so I have to go too.

The truck is so packed there's no room to move an inch. First nobody says a word. Dark eyes glare at us—damn outsiders! Then the men and women start talking again as if they'd only paused momentarily. Voices rise. They giggle, laugh. Their blanket of smells, which lifted when we got on, settles down again. Conversations zigzag back and forth between the travelers while the truck clears its throat, spits, sputters, then lurches ahead as if ready to topple any

moment. Firewood has to be poked into a small fur-
nace constantly, reducing the height of the rows. The
people seem to shrink.

I perch on Vati's hard knees, trying to make
myself light. I don't want to lean against his chest.
He's bound to be hurting from those broken ribs. I
look at the people, thin dark-haired men and women,
dirty as we are. Some speak a different dialect, but all
are jovial: We survived, we made it, they say. Joy
buoying their voices. Some are amputees, others
bandaged over much of their bodies, but they know
how to laugh, cackle. Scream hysterically.

In no time they've forgotten all about us, open
greasy bags and satchels that look good enough to
lick. They stack yellow block cheese, red-ripe salami,
loaves of bread bigger than babies on the box, which
they nudge with their knees. They saw the salami,
pass slabs around, chew off chunks of cheese, hack
the bread. Some men prop their elbows on Mutti's
box like it's a picnic table. Nobody offers us a bite,
not that I could eat anything. I have a big knot in my
throat.

Shhh, I say when the noise of the picnickers gets
too loud, *Nicht so laut.* I can't hear when she'll knock
on the wood.

We ride all day. Silhouettes of burned-out cities
rise and recede: black ruins against the cloudless
Bavarian sky like giant burnt hands poking out of the
earth. Vati names the cities, their former cathedrals,
monuments. He knows everything, even the small
towns we pass—now rubble and dust. One gets a lot
of attention. Finger pointing, neck craning, from the
people in the truck.

That's where it happened, over there. There....
Look at those chimneys....

But we didn't know, someone says. Only the educated folks knew. Kept it from us....

Every eye lands on Vati who stops talking, stares over their heads.

Knew what? I say.

No answer, but the mood changes. No more laughing. Vati's knees shift. He must have to pee-pee bad like I do, but the truck never stops. On it trundles through a scorched landscape. Huge woods are charcoal. Rivers have raw stone stumps where once big bridges used to span across. Bloated carcasses, human and animal, bob in murky water. Bomb craters are gigantic ulcers in ashen fields and look like moon lakes. Nearby fat buzzards huddle and only scatter when the truck approaches, leaving big white bones behind. Everywhere, the land is crying: So many men, women and children killed in the war....

Many long detours slow us down even more. Huff-puff-puff goes the stove that fires the engine. By then the people crouch on the floor, chins resting on the box, so much firewood's been used up. Mama hasn't woken up yet.

In the evening we arrive at another ruined city. Regensburg. The truck is tired, can hardly lumber to the train station. That's it for the night, says the driver. Everybody jumps off and finds a place to stretch out on the floor in the train station where already hundreds of other travelers are camping.

We have to hoist the box down. It's heavy, so we can only drag it a little ways. At last we're inside the train station too. Unlike other people, we don't have blankets to lie on. We lie on the dirty, cold stone floor and prop our heads against the coffin. It's greasy on top, smells of salami, pepperoni, cheese and pickles. That's our supper, those good smells. But it feels odd not being in the hallway at home. The floor here's just as hard, but there's no roof. The whole building has been bombed out, so the stars are visible.

I look for Mutti's bright light, that one she always talks about. But there's just pitch-black sky dotted with a few puny stars. Nothing moves. And my head and neck hurt from propping them against the coffin. I throw myself on top of the box, hug it tight, lick the grease spots. Isn't it enough, Mutti?

Wake up, wake up, wake up.

But she sleeps through everything.

The next day the truck creeps into Weiden where the family grave is. The whole Vierling history is entwined with this ancient town. An old couple awaits us, short, round, and identical, except for the length of their hair. Mutti's parents. I don't remember ever meeting them before. They act embarrassed, study their shapeless shoes. Tsk-tsk-tsk. Their faces are oatmeal, color and shape. They try to hug me, but I am a wild little animal—wary, scared, suspicious, ready to bite if not left alone. Don't touch—I will fight.

They sense it, spend their time comforting Ger, Hansi, Heda. Good, they need it.

I'm still waiting for Mutti to wake up. Until the last minute, I beg her to give us a sign, a knock, something to show she's through sleeping. I'm especially alert when I see some men in mismatched suits carry her box to a deep hole in the ground and begin to lower it into the earth. A pile of brown dirt rises next to the hole, and a red-faced priest is talking. Talking. I'm watching the hole.

Is this where all those dead mothers and children got raked into? Those burned up during the Magdeburg bombing? Mama's told me many times that I would've been one of them if she hadn't left East Germany. If she hadn't fled.

I inch as close to the pit as I can and look, holding my breath. No black skeletons down there, but the earth is moving. Worms have been hacked to pieces by the shovels of the grave diggers and wriggle, writhe.

Suddenly my face burns from shame. Thank God, it's not too late. I just remembered a conversation with Mutti. A week ago, a neighbor in Diessen said something to Mutti about dying. I overheard it and wrapped my arms around Mutti's waist. We're a perfect fit. She's so soft she feels like a big pillow. I press against it, inhale her smell, bury my face on her breast.

Mama, don't worry. If you ever die, I'll jump into the grave with you, I say.

No, you won't, she says, I won't let you.

But of course I will, I will, I will. What would I do without you?

Don't worry about it.

But I will jump in the grave with you. Really, truly. I promise.

Hush, nobody's going to die. Not for a long, long time!

That was then. So now I know what I must do.

Jump in the grave with her. Mama's not dead, of course. But what's going to happen when all that dirt's piled on her? She hates worms...I shiver thinking about them. But it's really not going to be hard, just hop in. Do it now before all that dirt gets shoveled on top of the box.

A man starts to shovel and Vati pulls me back.

I try to tear myself loose but he holds tight.

By now several more shovels of the rich dark dirt have fallen on my mother's coffin.

Let go, I scream and yank free.

I step to the edge of the hole again, look down. How deep it is, I can't see the bottom. But never mind. Mama's down there. I must jump. Will jump. Now.

More dirt has fallen. More, more.

Jump now. Right now.

But the dirt just keeps falling: plunk, plunk, plunk. It's dark snow being shoveled. More and more. The fresh dirt pile gets smaller. The hole fills up.

Now I jump, I say, hugging myself. Trembling. Now!

But I can't do it. I feel like those chopped-up earth worms—just bits and pieces of myself. Nothing works in me. My legs won't listen to my brain. I'm powerless, hurt, wooden, dead, but must jump in that grave. By then the dirt pile is gone; the coffin long since covered up. I'm aghast at what I've done: Oh, no. I broke my promise to Mutti, my only, dearest, beloved—I told her I would jump into the grave with her.

But I didn't do it. Didn't do it. Coward.

I sigh and sigh. Tonight when everybody's asleep I'll come back, dig up the dirt again, jump in.

The few worm pieces still lying around stop wriggling. I want to go to bed, I say to Vati.

Now? It's only three o'clock.

Yes, I'm so tired.

Poor child, my grandmother says, leads me a long way through rubble streets to where they live—a tiny walk-up apartment with cracks in the walls, decorated with sick browns of all shades. Waxy cloths, sagging furniture. Musty old odors. There are gray doilies, moth-eaten afghans, probably knitted by my mother when she was a girl.

But nothing smells like my Mutti. I sink in a featherbed, force myself to dream. It's a sunny day. We children and Mutti are at the Ammersee swimming. Mutti, beautiful with young legs, dives in. Paddles gracefully out into the dark blue water, and straight into a clump of leeches. They descend on her, suck on her, weigh her down. She keeps swimming but has to struggle more and more, and I'm watching from the shore as she's pulled under—

Wake up. I do. It's the middle of the night and that strange old couple—my grandparents—are in bed with me. I scoot to the edge of the mattress, cling to it. Claw it. Don't want to touch them.

Anyway, must get up, go to the cemetery, jump in the grave with my Mutti. Save her from drowning in the dirt. Right now! Move!

But I don't know the way, and the house is a dark cave, and cozy from the warmth and smells of so many people crammed into such a small space. And I'm so weak from hunger.

Feigling. Coward.

CHAPTER 3

Dinner of Ashes

Back in Diessen, Mutti's death-generated gifts of food run out quickly. Then there's nothing to eat, again. The grocery stores have all been bombed out or looted. They're locked and boarded up like battened-down beach cottages before a hurricane.

People live off what food they have stored in their cellars. But after six war years, that's all gone. Next is eat what's growing in the garden. But with my mother gone and with my father leaving the house for days at a time to roam the woods—looking for mushrooms and berries, he claims, but I don't see him bringing any home—there's nobody to grow a garden.

We kids wander around Diessen and the fields surrounding it. We poke in ditches, gutters, dig our fingers through caked earth in search of a potato or carrot a farmer has overlooked. We pick over the wheat fields already gleaned by other folks. Peel bark off birch trees, which isn't bad. Nibble the tips of fir branches, which are tasty in the spring. Cram bunches of young grass in our mouths. Suck on pebbles, snack on dandelion leaves and their blooms. Their stems are milky and make our mouths break out in sores but fill our tummies. For a while.

Soon we sport rashes that never heal. Colds last years. Minor cuts we pick up running wild all day turn into craters that gape and ooze. Vati pulls out needle and thread when the tips of his fingers crack and his thumbs split wide open. He threads the needle and sews his torn skin together but we run when he comes after us. Ever since he doused Heda's foot with iodine after she cut herself, and by mistake poured some acid on her and burned a palm-sized piece of her skin, we've been leery of his doctoring.

He knows just enough medicine to be dangerous.

But he doesn't chase us. He knows sooner or later we'll drag home to see if any food has shown up. Never does, of course. But we come and go as we please, still wearing all our clothes and never bathing. What six-year-old would think of making a fire to heat water for a bath?

Not me.

No extra wood anyway, but Heda heats water sometimes. Tastes better warm than cold, especially when bark bits float in it. The end result, a gritty gray broth, reminds you of Mama's various water soups.

But to strip off all our layers of ragged clothes and wash ourselves? Are you crazy?

By then the clothes are our armor. Our second skin. The thinner we get, the more clothes we pile on.

Ours and Mama's, and whatever other rags we find. As if the heaps of dirty clothes that by now are a breeding ground for lice and bedbugs could give us the nourishment we don't have. But they keep us alive. For the time being.

I wear torn blankets as capes, swath my head in scraps, trail tattered towels as scarves, suck on my mother's dirty old pink slip. It helps. Still I feel hunger pains. It's years and years of endless hunger, though maybe it's only a decade.

But it feels like centuries. There's always a wild raging animal chewing on my insides. It gets worse when I go to the bathroom. It's then that wild animal, which gnaws steadily but bearably the rest of the time, wakes up, stretches, grows. Growls, pounces. Roars and gnaws with its sharp teeth at every one of my organs. I scream. It's this unbearable pain. I almost faint from the agony. Sometimes I do.

Fainting dulls the pain: The hunger animal's satisfied again for the moment.

What makes those hunger pains worse is my father's inability to face the condition we're in. He has four starving kids. And yes, he does tramp through the woods a lot. But why doesn't he bring home a dead deer more often? He found one a couple of weeks ago. It had been dead so long, its hide was black-purple, fuzzy and studded with green flies. But never mind the smell and the maggots. Just scrape them off and dig in. Rotten deer meat's so good. Gives you something to chew on, gets the stomach working again.

You can suck on your fist just so long before you draw blood.

Finally Vati has a good idea. He's watched us kids get weaker each day. By now we know if we stop running and just lie on the floor, the hunger beast stays quiet. All we need's a sip of water now and then. Suck on our bloody knuckles. Lie there, wait.

Fact is Vati's been wasting his time scratching around for food. He has neither the talent for it nor the patience. He isn't good at begging either, or at wheeling and dealing on the black market. When he takes an oil painting to trade for a loaf of bread, he only gets half. Of course, on the way home, he always comes across some kids worse off than us, gaunt skeletons in rags lying in the gutter. At least we have a roof and four walls, no matter how ugly, how icy. But other kids have less.

So by the time Vati comes home, he only has a couple of slices of bread left, which Hansi snatches, crams down.

Whatever else my father's been able to scrounge up goes to my sisters. I'm just a small bundle in the corner. It's not that he forgets about me. But in times of hunger, the kids that clamor most get the bite.

By then I'm beyond needing food anyway. At a certain point starvation takes you by the hand, sinks you into half-sleep. You just want to stay warm and still, wait, just wait. Wait for the lake.

Vati's got to do something. In despair, he goes into partnership with someone who's fantastic at black marketeering, a tall beautiful blonde woman from Cologne, Julie. He's known her ever since before the war, when he had his own company. When he was on his way to become the most famous engineer and inventor in the country. The world. When all things were still possible.

Now Julie is a widow. Her husband who was part of a motorcycle brigade was killed by Balkan guerrillas. Shot between the eyes. Until then Julie was a great success herself. The only daughter of a furrier from High Street in the heart of bustling Cologne, she married a thriving import-export salesman who took her on a lavish honeymoon cruise to Cape Town.

Her shoulder-length, wheat-colored hair fluttering in the breeze on deck and her fashionable gowns were the talk of the luxury liner.

After the honeymoon came four kids in quick succession, all blond, blue-eyed boys. Stair steps. Then the war destroyed the family business, her home, her husband. Yet it couldn't destroy her flair. In the midst of total starvation and ruins, she's still a fashion plate. While other women wear drab rags, she wears hers with a flower, a shimmering belt, bits of lace. Rhinestones. When other women don men's work overalls and galoshes, she takes an old man's suit, rips the seams, sews the cloth panels into a tailored skirt and jacket, and wears that "ensemble" in different variations for the next 15 years—the only time I knew her.

She varies the length of the skirt. Reverses the collar. Sews on pockets. Changes buttons. Takes out a panel, adds pleats here, there. Ruffles, ruches, smocking....

She isn't the only woman who makes her own wedding dress by hand, stitch for stitch, right after the war. But she's the only one who patches one together out of squares cut from other dresses and sewn together so seamlessly that in the end, the dress looks like the latest Paris creation. Julie looks stunning: Her hair lies in thick wheat coils. Her blue eyes sparkle. Her peach skin is flawless.

But *ach du lieber!* Oma's unhappy again. Julie's a step up from Barbara, of course, but only one step. Oma yells at Vati: Why can't you find someone from our society?

But he's desperate, wants to get back to his inventions, not spend all his time looking for edible roots, hoping a deer will croak, so he can drag it home.

The wedding takes place less than a year after Barbara's death. But Vati cracks a smile. He's convinced that if one broken family can live on a bare minimum, two broken families, united into one, can do much better.

Wrong. First, we haven't lived since Barbara died. We only just clung on white-knuckled. Second, now with eight kids to feed, the bark, the grass clumps no matter how enticing, the wild berries and occasional crusts of dry bread are really inadequate.

But how it relieves Vati to turn his starved kids over to Julie who thinks surely there's got to be more food in Bavaria than in bombed-out Cologne.

Is she in for a shock. There's nothing but barren dirt and barkless trees in our poor yard, our sad house. The most valuable household items have long since been traded for crumbs.

And what a time she has, trying to peel us out of our layers of rotting, stinking clothes, and scrub us. We cringe at the sight of a washrag. Combing out our matted hair and delousing us is another big battle, but help arrives.

Oh, finally, finally: real food again.

Since our house sits on a hill and is embraced by thick woods on all sides, it's a perfect observation point for the occupation. Soon the front door bursts open: An American captain with several enlisted men storm the house, guns drawn, and search every nook and cranny.

But there are no resistance fighters hiding any-where. There's nothing but a bunch of hollow-eyed kids with bellies swollen from hunger. Vati's taken off again, as usual, this time for longer. Hiking in the Alps, probably. With his good looks that only intensi-fy the thinner he gets, some Austrian farm girl high in the mountains who's managed to hide a few goats is sure to invite him to a hearty meal. Or more.

Meanwhile all of Germany has been drawn, quar-tered and divvied up by the four victorious armies —the Americans, the British, the French and the Russians. At the moment Diessen is in the hands of the Americans. Our house is chosen as headquar-ters. A cheerful American flag flaps in the wind from our attic window.

If Mutti could only see this. America has come to us.

Our bedrooms are assigned to the soldiers. Julie and we eight kids are shoved into one room and held there like criminals for hours. What's our crime? They don't say, but eye us suspiciously.

Later the soldiers fan out to secure the rest of the area. They capture Diessen and the lake, come back loaded. Some have wristwatches sparkling on their forearms all the way up to their elbows. Others swing cackling white chickens by their orange feet and toss them into our kitchen sink. They aim their guns at Julie, make her wring the chickens' necks and cook them along with armloads of vegetables they have "liberated" from the surrounding farms. The smell of real food being cooked brings tears to our eyes.

Oh, oh. The aroma of potatoes boiling! Real red cabbage simmering with stewed apples! The perfume of a real chicken slowly turning golden-brown in a big pan in the old cast-iron oven that's sat cold and silent for too long. It's heavenly. We kids rally, splash cold water in our faces, paste our disheveled hair down with spit. Each breath of those delicious odors wafting into our noses and from there into our lungs is paradise.

My mouth waters. How I lick my cracked lips in anticipation. Quickly we scurry about, set the dining room table with our best dishes, cram dandelions into a glass jar for a centerpiece for those wonderful clean-shaven men who have extorted whatever food supplies still exist in the farthest corners of town. Our heroes. They even squeezed food from the abbeys and monasteries nearby.

Can you believe our good luck?

Just look at everything: Cherry jam glistens in glass jars like rubies. Perfect little pickles wink like emeralds. Butter? Is that real butter? Oh, has anything ever looked better than a hunk of creamy butter? It's pure golden. A chunk of sun.

Excitedly we kids take our places. The Americans have forgiven us for being who we are and smile at our eagerness; now they're sure Julie isn't trying to poison them. As a precaution they station a soldier in the kitchen, weapon drawn, to watch her. They make her taste everything she cooks.

Lucky her.

Finally the feast begins.

The chairs are pulled out, and the captain and his men sit. We watch how they lower their taut behinds on our rickety chairs. What an honor. Ahhh. How nice, they're here in our house, have come to save us. We're the chosen.

We kids are planted where we're told to be. One of us, trembling from excitement, behind each chair, so we can serve our soldiers. And later bring them more food when they want it. We watch in awe as they load their plates. So much food. And how pretty everything is, the contrast of colors of the meat and vegetables on the plates. The heavenly smells that envelop us.

Like happy hawks we watch every move the soldiers make. Anticipate every delicious morsel. Savor every bite along with them. Tears flood our eyes when our own handsome soldier lifts his fork, starts digging in, tucks a forkful into his mouth.

Ah-oh. Now he's tasting some chicken. He's chewing it with his strong white teeth, of which he has many. Wow. But, please, not so fast, we want to scream. Slow, chew slow. And now he's eating a potato. Some cabbage. Oh, oh. What pretty little green peas he's spearing. Must be so delicious. Sweet. Tasty. Oh.

Now the bread. A big bite of bread with real butter.

Our soldier put that into his mouth! And now another bite—Ah! We sigh. Lick our lips again. Chew when the soldiers do. Swallow when they swallow. We moan, but not loudly. That would get us banished from the room. We would die if we couldn't be part of this.

Ach, ach, jaja. These wonderful delicious-smelling men eat all that wonderful delicious-smelling food. And they're so nice, kind. Smile so much, laugh too. We haven't heard anyone laugh so much in forever, so we're stunned.

Why are they laughing?

We keep following their forks. We watch their hands, arms. Turn our heads so we can see their strong jaws chewing. We imagine those wonderful tastes. Wish we could be their lips, tongues, teeth, throats, stomachs—just once.

If a soldier drops a morsel, we fling ourselves on it. Lick the spot on the floor where the pea landed, the piece of cabbage dropped. Then scramble back to our proper places.

And oh. How we pray there's enough food for all the men. So they won't get angry and demand more. Or clean every speck off their plates. So we wait, wait and are not disappointed. There's enough. The smiles continue. These young gods in their starched uniforms with their gleaming teeth get out their cigarettes. We haven't seen anyone smoke for years. There's no tobacco anymore in Germany. Old men in town smoke weeds and straw, and cough until they rattle.

But not these gods. They smoke real cigarettes and ask Julie to brew the most delicious dark drink—

coffee. Real coffee. What a lovely word. The rich brown liquid sparkles in their cups. It's the most beautiful color in the world.

The gods rock back in our chairs, talk in a language that sounds musical though intelligible. Only their lower jaws move. They smoke cigarette after cigarette, slurp coffee, while we're trembling with anticipation. Soon, soon.

And finally, finally the soldiers finish, go back to securing the village. To liberating more loot. Then we eat.

Miracle of miracle. We each get what's left on our soldier's plate, all of it. Groaning we fall over chicken bones and gristle and devour everything. If we're lucky, we find a delicious left-over bread crust, suck up the dregs of black coffee, slurp up gravy. Oh heavenly! Mixed in with the gravy remnants are the best cigarette ashes you can imagine.

We sling everything down. Lick the plates spotless, spoons, forks, knives too—anything that has a speck of food on it. Yum-yum.

We are in pure heaven. Scour the floor over and over for bits of food, cram any cigarette butts we find outside into our mouths. For dessert we enjoy all the pink wads of chewing gum stuck under the table. It's all so, so delicious. And how we fight over the dirty pots in the kitchen, slobber over the stove, suck on the napkins the soldiers used. Clutch the old table cloth, hug the chairs our gods sat in. Kiss where they sat.

We're lucky. Finally, real food again. Looks like we're going to make it.

The feasting goes on for many glorious weeks, for many incredible months when we live only for the evening galas, when we pray that maybe today our soldier will leave a little extra gravy on his plate. One whole green bean. A piece of potato. Maybe our soldier will bite into a piece of roast, find it too chewy, too much fat. Take it out of his mouth, place it on the edge of his plate! Please. What a treat to get a morsel that's already pre-chewed. A bone of our own has us in ecstasy for days. We crunch it with our teeth if they're not too loose, if they haven't fallen out, suck the marrow, gnaw on the bone gently. Make it last, last.

We sleep, dreaming of gristle.

While the Americans live with us, we still suffer from rickets, scurvy and trench mouth with its craterlike ulcers that erupt in our swollen and bleeding gums. But at least, our malnutrition isn't getting worse.

As long as we get to lick out those supper plates, we manage to hang on.

Even the worms we have don't bother us as much during this time. Of course at night they still make us itch. And in the morning we find long brown ones whipping around in our underpants, but the little boys' swollen bellies actually shrink.

We're all so happy. So grateful.

CHAPTER 4

Blood Games

J ulie's in her element. She went to school in
Switzerland, knows how many seconds it
takes to whip up a luscious lemon meringue,
where delicate finger bowls go on a table, how to
lightly starch fluffy gauze curtains. Every day she
jumps out of bed at 6 AM and dresses in her finest
black rag suit, whose collar she turns yet again,
whose stains she scrubs passionately. She presses it
with a damp cloth and an iron that hibernates on the
back of the stove.

It only works if there's a fire.

But never mind. Julie acts as if she's running a
first-class hotel and restaurant. While she's forced to
be the cook and maid for the occupation soldiers
who've turned her home into a barracks, she's a bundle of cheerful energy. Rushes from room to room
picking up dirty soldier underwear, whisks up fancy
trays with finger sandwiches, serves them every

afternoon to the gods. They snore with their muddy boots on top of the sheets, play cards all day, toss trash on the floor, fling dirty shirts at her. There's always a lot of garbage to wade through and mountains of laundry, yet Julie has a big smile pasted on her face: Hope's in the air.

Inside it's different.

First to go is her memory. She can't remember the children's names and calls all of us from the oldest to the youngest whenever she wants just one:

Heda-Hansi-Heini-Ger—a breath—Rudi-Erika-Paul-Joachim. On good days, she stops on the name she wants. On bad days, she just keeps calling names. Over and over. A broken record, but with a smile.

We kids get smart, tune her out. For when we come running, things only get worse, especially for us girls. We're the chamber maids, the kitchen help, the *Putzfrauen*. I have to wash dozens of socks each day, kneeling in the dank basement. Piles of pee sheets. The little boys aren't house-broken yet. So I use harsh soap, if there's any, and cold water in buckets and a brush. Drape the sheets on branches, hang the socks on a line.

That's the easy part.

The hard part is the mending.

The sheets just get patched, which takes forever but isn't too hard. But the socks are the real killers. Since they're all ancient, except for the American soldiers' socks, they have to be darned constantly. But the holes are bigger than fists and growing. And the mending yarn is just unraveled bits and pieces from moth-eaten sweaters and breaks all the time.

The needles are dull, rusty. The basket of torn socks and underwear grows like a giant mushroom every day. Meanwhile the boys run shoeless outside and tear their socks even more.

Boys will be boys. Girls will be slaves.

I bow my head, learn to weave without a loom. Run straight lines of yarn across the abysses, weave other threads across in a grid at 90 degrees. Have to make brand-new material to close the gaping holes. All the socks, sweaters, and pants are more mended material than original fabric. I darn the mended places a second, third, fourth, fifth, sixth time. And our clothes are rags that need patching. Towels are only threads and fringes, and must be stitched together time and again.

An endless task for a seven-year-old girl—me. But how I try, desperately. And I think, think. Why? Why?

My older sisters have chores too.

There's the nonstop dishwashing. Dishes are always stacked to the ceiling. But why do we have to wash the dinner plates? After our feasts with the American soldiers they sparkle. And why does Julie uses separate plates, some for salads, others for bread—and all those glasses? Am I glad she's only one step up from Barbara. Whatever would she put me through if she were real society?

So many, many dirty dishes. First always it's find some wood, roam around outside till you discover a small tree, chop it down with a dull axe, hack it to pieces. Tote the wood into the dark kitchen, heat up the old brass kettle, green from age, with water. Wash every damn dish. Easy if there's soap. Hard without it. No soap makes the water slime. Then rinse dishes in cold water, dry dishes with rags dirtier than the dishes were to begin with.

Do that job over and over several times each day. A dozen soldiers plus eight kids means lots of dishes. The work's never ever done. But the dirtier the kitchen and dishes, the utensils and what few furnishings haven't been sold on the black market, the more Julie's determined to have a spotless house.

A nice hotel for our "guests."

So just more work for me. I can't run away as fast as the others when she calls—the result of my rickets. Hour after hour I bend over the grimy kitchen sink. My back burns. Then comes mopping the unfinished wooden floors, which look good and clean for only a few seconds. As soon as they dry, they look filthy again. And are. The dirt is ingrained.

While I scrub away, getting splinters in my hands, Julie walks from room to room, screams: Why isn't this done? Cleaned? Polished? Sparkling?

When I have finally stashed away clean forks and spoons, she dumps out the drawers—wasn't neat enough. Rips my mending apart—not done right. Yanks all the clean sheets and pillow cases out of the closet and onto the floor—not folded to perfection. You lazy good-for-nothing cripple!

I know I'm no good. Promise to do better and try, really try. It's clear that Julie's hurting. The poverty, the strange men occupying her house, Vati off again, leaving her to cope with the boys who're running wild. It's getting on her nerves. On top of that, the smallest girl, me, does such a lousy job.

School's started up again. And wouldn't you know it? That useless little girl wants to go to school. Begs to go, can't wait to hobble out of the house every morning. Runs, runs! When she thinks she's out of sight.

And if Julie doesn't watch her carefully, she even has the gall to stick her nose into a book after school. As if there isn't work to be done: beds to make, laundry, wood to chop, rooms to sweep.

Julie is getting frantic with the way everything's getting shabbier and shabbier in the house, filthier and filthier, but still she smiles. Though now it takes a while for her smile to appear each morning. Then without warning the American soldiers leave, and her only food source dries up. No more delicious plates to lick, no more nourishing pots to scrape out. No more pretend-waiting on our nice "guests."

Now nothing.

That afternoon I find Julie in the backyard. She's sitting on the brown grass, has a blouse and slip tied in a bundle, looks like she'd been trying to run away, then stopped because she didn't know where to. Diessen is wallowing in widows like her. Frightened refugees huddle on corners, asking for handouts. Nobody has anything to eat.

Sure, other women have fewer children. Their life's easier. But nobody will take Julie in. She is stuck, and she's just found out she's pregnant. Hans has come home for a short while. Instead of taking precautions he's done *this* to her, she tells me.

What should I do? Her eyes flicker as she probes the earth with a long rusty nail.

She looks like a trapped deer and I shrug: I don't know.

She starts crying, and I can tell she has no idea who I am.

Let's go back in the house, I'll make you some "tea" (hot water with birch bark or linden leaves), I say.

No. Don't you understand? I can't. I'm so ashamed.

Of course I understand. *Finally there's someone I can talk to. Ask questions.* I'm ashamed, too, whenever I think about *it*.

Think about what?

Dachau.

What are you talking about?

I flinch under her tone. But didn't you just say…?

Because I only have one piece of lettuce! And company's coming this afternoon.

I sigh, sigh. Why don't you tell them we have nothing? But I know she would never do that. Unlike other hungry families, we can never admit we're starving. We're half society. Always when somebody stops by we have to pretend we just ate. Then ply the visitor with the few potatoes we have that are supposed to last us the rest of the week. We have to act like we have lots: Here, help yourself. Go on, take the rest home…while we're dying from hunger.

That's the way Julie treats company—always with a smile, while we kids run outside to hide our tears. And we can't ever wear dirty clothes with holes. Oh no. Everything's got to be clean and mended.

It's so hard to be poor when you can't enjoy it.

Why don't I look for some nettles? I say, with a sigh and pat Julie on the arm. Old nettle leaves are tough and sting like wasps, but the new ones are tasty. And then I'll fix you some "tea," yes? You'll feel better after you eat something—

I don't mind being hungry, she says, head hanging. It's not having anything to offer when somebody comes, that's unbearable. Again she digs in the earth.

Maybe the boys can steal something for our company?

I sent them already. That's where the piece of lettuce is from. But it's too much. Really. I can't, I really can't—I won't....No more babies, you understand? Julie trembles, looks past me. I notice that her wheat-colored hair has wide bands of gray. Her peach skin is puckered around the eyes. Her mouth, full and red just a year ago, is a colorless thread. How old is she?

Later I ask Heda, who says: 32.

The next day Julie's in the small hospital down the street. We kids just carry on like we used to when Barbara died. Wasn't long ago, so we know the routine. Scrounge for something to cram in your mouth, anything you can get your hands on, all right? Wear all the clothes you can find. It's like a long vacation, ha ha. Nobody makes you do anything. No bath, no combing hair. Go to bed at midnight. Just run around, scream, hit who gets in your way. In my case, get my school books out of hiding and read. Read.

While she's in the hospital, I don't wash a single dish, scrub a sock or mop a floor. No mending! I run around without shoes, rip my socks and clothes. Free, free. I read all night. Then I'm summoned to Julie's bedside.

Guiltily I traipse down Krankenhausweg to the

small hospital that still has scars from the bombing. Inside, sheets are stiff and new. There are real towels, clean floors, ammonia smells. The nuns have put Julie on the second floor where I tiptoe, knock.

I expect to get yelled at, but Julie's all smiles.

She's sitting up in a bed that's decorated in white and crimson. The white is from the sheets and the crimson from the big puddle of blood between her legs. Julie has no idea who I am, doesn't ramble through the usual litany of children's names. Instead, she asks me to sit on the side of her bed: Play patty-cake with me.

Sure. I sit down. She dips her hands in the fresh blood and claps them together, then against my hands. I play with her, so relieved she's not screaming at me for being lazy. I'll play all day with her, every day, if it makes her happy.

In a few weeks, she's home again. The yelling starts again, the screeching, but the new baby never comes. Next time Julie isn't so lucky. She has three more kids, all boys, before she finally discovers a sure-fire method to stop having babies.

But before that, the impossible pattern of her trying to get the house back in order and finding a way to feed us kids continues. When the struggle gets too hard, she has another nervous breakdown, which removes her from us for however long the nuns keep her as they try to make her better.

Breakdowns after breakdowns come like waves.

But those many hospital stays are my salvation. Life is bearable when Julie's sick.

Still every night, I crawl into my narrow bed and

sob. I hug the pillow, muffle my cries. When Ger comes to bed—she, Heda and I share a room with three cots—I beg her to let me slide in with her. She doesn't want me to, but I bribe her. I'll do your chores.

OK, just don't touch me, crybaby.

I know. I'm a crybaby, a coward. Nervous, embarrassed. Ugly too, and with so many questions. But after Ger's fallen asleep, I inch my foot over, touch my little toe to hers, feel her skin. Reminds me of Mama. I feel a moan form in my heart, fill my chest, wanting out. Out.

But I suppress it, all but a whimper: Is this what life is supposed to be? Nothing but work and hunger when Julie's home—and guilt and hunger when she's in the hospital?

Touching Ger's toe helps though. I just pretend she's Mutti. Where are you? I ask the darkness. Why can't I wrap my arms around you, sniff you like I used to? Inhale you? Warm myself in your nearness?

I cuddle close to Ger, but she smells like me—bad. Still, her dirty foot is better than nothing. I haven't had a hug, a pat, a good word in so long.

Not even a kind look. Or just one without a sting in it.

Julie never gives me any of those things. Never thanks me, never just lets me be. Not even when she's in the hospital again and asks me to run home and bring her all the letters from the priest.

Don't you dare let Vati see them, she says, turning pink. Looking like a girl from before the war; I've seen pictures.

I bring her the letters. She clutches them to her chest, rubs, caresses them. Kisses them. I watch her lavish such care on some dumb sheets written on in black ink. It's just paper with writing on, that's all. I'm so jealous I can't stand it. I hurt....

Vati's different, naturally. He dishes out affection to us kids, but too much.

I'm not his wife. Doesn't he understand?

Sure, I want a hug, but just a hug. Not those long drawn-out kisses on the mouth.

CHAPTER 5

Bed of Bugs

Up! Up! On Saturdays Vati wakes everyone at 6 AM, tucks some bread or a couple boiled potatoes in his back pocket, then marches all of us children into the woods. Maybe he sees signs of Julie's unraveling again and wants us out of the way before some real tragedy occurs. Or maybe he's lonely or feels guilty. He does love the outdoors. *Die Natur.* Being fit. But we kids hate those forced marches in the wild. Having to walk nonstop for the next two days. How can we get out of the torture?

One look at Vati's face tells you, don't even try.

So we trot, first down the hill away from the cold house with our stomachs growling, our feet hurting already. Everyone's shoes are passed down. By the time they get to me, they have big holes so I stuff cardboard and newspaper in them. That works fine until it rains, when the wet road makes the newspaper clump and fall through the holes. Water splashes in. That cools down the toes that are pinched and blistery. But in fall and winter it freezes my feet.

Fortunately most times, it doesn't rain on our forced marches, but our feet still suffer. At the bottom of the hill, we trudge wearily right in the direction of Raisting, a neighboring small town where maybe we'll find an apple tree. Maybe we'll come across a nice garbage heap.

You have to say that for Vati: He's very good about letting us stop and shake down trees or stir around in garbage piles. It's the only shopping we ever do and costs nothing. On the contrary, we find the most wonderful free stuff: amber-colored liquids in dusty bottles, which we gulp down. Old medicines maybe. Bitter brews of some type. But it's something to drink and who cares, as long as it goes down without coming back up?

We love to dig deep in the dirt, find other wondrous things: door knobs, caked and torn underpants, pieces of shiny metal that we give Vati. He collects nails, screws, nuts, tinfoil, old keys. Mattress coils, curtain rods, rusty cans and lots of other useful stuff. We get on our knees, comb through the garbage and slime with our fingers for matchboxes, rubber squares, broken pencils, rusty lids. Hair curlers, rope, broken cups, holey pots. That's how we get our toys. We find a little broken car, a doll's arm. A teddybear head without eyes. More next time.

We could spend all day poking in the trash piles, but Vati moves on. And when he's ready to go, we better hop to it. Not much farther down the road, apple trees beckon. Chomping on wormy apples—

just close your eyes and don't look so you won't see the worms—halts our hunger for a while. We pee behind the bushes.

Then on we trudge, kilometer after kilometer.

At lunch, if we haven't irritated him by whining, Vati lets us sink down in the shade of ancient elms. He shares the bread or potatoes like the scientist he is: Exact portions are cut with an old pocketknife. The smallest kids get to pick their rations first, the oldest kids come last. Fair is fair. By then we've made trades among ourselves, offering to carry a little brother who's crying, if we get his bread. The older boys just raise a fist behind Vati's back, shake it and end up with two portions. I hate to get hit.

I don't know why it still hurts after I've been hit so often.

Then it's off again, many more kilometers to cover. To the ends of the earth, it seems like. It's great when we find some walnuts on the way. Or dewy blackberry patches, a field of wild mushrooms. Vati says, taste all mushrooms. If they're bitter, spit them out. You'll be fine. Bitter means they're poisonous.

He's right. Nobody ever dies. But often some of the brothers get sick and vomit for the next few hours.

No problem. Go to it. Spit up. Get it out of your system. Do whatever you need to but hurry. Vati doesn't wait around. You got diarrhea? Be sure to run fast afterwards; catch up.

There are many picturesque small hills and several steeper ones in that part of Bavaria, called Voralpen (Piedmont). From the distance their green tops look smoky. Below them, crystal-clear lakes reflect the sun. Some lakes are ringed by mountain ranges dating back to a time when glaciers occupied the area. As they melted, the lakes puddled. So we always have plenty of water as we put one series of hills behind us, then another. And another. Vati's always first, then come the older kids, the middle ones to which I belong, then the smaller ones.

We never follow a path or road. That would be too easy. No, Vati bulldozes through thickets and dense woods. Up one side of a mountain, down the other. Up the next, down again and so on.

At first we talk among ourselves, the boys always rebellious but mumbling low enough that Vati can't hear them. But they mutter over and over: Can't wait to grow up, fly the coop. Out of here. Just watch me. Damn fucking yes, I'll be gone. Gone!

We three girls know we're stuck, especially me, the youngest. Just the thought of leaving Julie is awful. What would she do without at least one slave? She'd be condemned to constant mental illness, not just to bouts of it.

By Saturday evening, all talk stops. All the brave mumbling fizzles out. We're so weary and hungry, want to fall down somewhere and die. Get it over with.

But Vati keeps attacking birch tree copses, fir stands, and thorny brush. He's a fast-moving machine. Bristles whip us in the face. Brambles and branches suck our blood. Undisturbed, he points out yellow ladyslippers, the shimmering black fruit of bella donna, wild ferns with Latin names *this* long, and mossy streams overhung by rare grasses, where we long to soak our raw feet.

Our blisters are crab-apple size.

But oh. There's no mercy. On and on we have to jog, run, crawl, creep. If you fall behind you get lost. There are still many places that harbor land mines. We all have classmates with an arm or leg missing. Their parents didn't care where they walked in the woods. But our Vati knows where it's safe. Just keep up with his crazy pace. His insane charging up the mountains. His victory over vicious vines, timber jumbles, brush mazes.

When we get a moment's rest, the boys brag of running away, but nothing ever comes of it. Where would they run to? The country lies in ruins. And starving at home is better than starving in a strange place. We know how we're treated by family—bad enough. Wouldn't strangers be worse?

When it gets dark, Vati becomes human again, lets out his breath, finds us a good place to sleep. Oh, how wonderful if he discovers a barn full of hay. We fall into the fragrant dry grass like boulders, topsy-turvy, let the hay mounds embrace us, sleep until he rousts us early Sunday.

Most times the barns are bare. Or grumpy farmers chase us with pitchforks and vicious dogs. *Raus-raus, fort-fort.* Get along. Away with you trash. Then Vati picks out the prettiest patch of lawn or a field that's just been cut. The grass is still wet. Silently we rake it together with our hands, make pallets out of it, crawl into the damp mounds. A pitch-dark night falls. The stars hide. I don't blame them. Wish I could.

We lie in a circle, all of us kids and Vati, feet touching, our heads radiating out. The brothers and Vati snore in a contest. My two sisters fall fast asleep and

I'm wide awake and suffering. Worrying.

Why? Why can't I be too tired to care, like the rest of them?

Why can't I be a little wood animal, curl up and rest? Snuggle in cozy under the odors of cow manure and boys' farts?

But no. I have to analyze everything, think about the whole wide world. Mostly I think about people. What they've done in my country. Why did they stuff people just like themselves into ovens? Burn them to death, then never say one word about it?

Why?

Whenever I ask Heda about the concentration camps, she says: Don't ask so many dumb questions.

But I have to.

Oh, when you get older, you'll stop asking. Wait and see, she says. Just you wait and see.

But it's been a year or longer since I first heard about Dachau, which isn't far away from Diessen. It's incredible what people did to other people there. But it happened. And I get older every day and still the same questions come. They pounce on me, make my heart race like a trip hammer. Why-why-why?

Why didn't someone stop what was going on?

Why didn't Vati stop it?

Some day when I can find the right moment, I'll ask him. I won't be a coward all my life. None of the other kids are cowards. They exist day by day, eat what they can, elbow for space, fight for their life. I'm ashamed to be different, but must try to fit in better, be a regular, snot-nosed, post-war German kid. Daring and tough.

❦ ❦ ❦

BED OF BUGS

One of those late afternoons when dinner preparations should be going on: everywhere in the neighborhood sounds of mothers rushing around, backdoors slamming, pots clanging, as they scrape something together to feed their families.

It's quiet at our place. There's nothing to scrape together. No pots are tolling—a sound prettier than church bells ringing. There's no running water to wash vegetables with, no sounds of the chopping of onions, no smells of cooking anything. Julie is home from the hospital though. She's fine for the moment. But her pale cheeks have high red circles from where she's propped her face on her worn hands. All day long. She's subdued, too tired even to call us *Kinder*. Not one of us, not even me. No Heda, Hansi, Heini, Ger, Rudi, Erika...litany this time.

I look in on her. She sags like a gravestone sunk into the ground. Her silence is worse than her screaming. I tiptoe back out of the cold dark kitchen. Always our yard is a haven with its outbuildings, huge trees, a secluded back lawn. I wander through the grass that's never cut in search of young dandelions. Juicy clover. Maybe I can concoct something for supper. Pick enough for all of us to munch on. Make a crisp salad.

Rudi and Ger call me. They're closest in age to me, so we're often together: Come back here and play with us.

Supper's quickly forgotten; hunger is on hold. I sprint back to the farthest corner of the yard where they are running around naked. Their bony, smooth bodies jump through the waist-high grass like albino deer. Ger is eight, Rudi seven and a half, I'm seven.

They have invented a new game, something nice for a change, I think, and can't wait to join in. All the other games we play are mean. It's as if the hunger has robbed us not only of body fat, but also of goodness. I remember a long time ago, Heda and Ger had dolls. Mutti used to tell us bedtime stories, Ger and I played *Haus* with little huts we built from sticks and bark pieces before we had to eat them. We used to make daisy chains. These days we eat them too.

Now we play only bad games, cruel games. Nasty games. We know it's wrong but can't help ourselves. In summer, we pee into an old teapot and offer it to other kids to drink. Do we laugh when we see them grimace, retch and spit.

In winter, we poke big holes into the ice in the lake, lace twigs across the openings, brush fine snow on top, then inspect the "holes." Looks perfect. We wait expectantly for other kids to walk toward our trap and step on the flimsy coverings. When they fall in, get a leg doused in the freezing water, scream, shiver, turn blue, we laugh uproariously.

The more mischief we cause, the more we laugh. When we see Hansi skate across the lake wearing nothing but underpants and a shirt, whose soggy tails flap in the wind, his legs purple while his pants are drying on a bush nearby, we laugh even louder, but only after we're out of sight. Fool fell into that really big hole we made. Aren't we clever?

Our games get more vicious.

A neighbor down the street is like us—without work, money, food. But he's not like Vati who keeps on "inventing" like he did before the war as if nothing happened. Back then he had science labs, work-shops, a factory, materials, instruments, books, graph paper, every tool imaginable. A staff. Now all he has is a single slide rule and all the rusty metal pieces we dig out of the trash.

Meanwhile the neighbor has branched out into a new field. He's now breeding fine rabbits, the rarest of breeds only, in an elaborate shed. Next to mouse-colored rabbits with scruffy pelts, he keeps beautiful Angoras with the longest, silkiest black or white hair in a row of cages and has come up with an even newer breed that will soon be very valuable. Very pure. He keeps the males strictly separated from the females, has all kinds of locks and bars for security reasons, and charts for when the mating is best. A long list of customers already waiting for the next litter is posted, with more names added each day. Profits are sure to come in, a big cash flow any day now. The neighbor and his family depend on the money that's soon to come in.

But when he's gone, we track down his little son. Hey you, kid. Want to play with us?

His face lights up. Yes, please, please. Playing with us older and tougher kids is an honor for him. He can hardly believe his good luck.

All right. But first let's let your rabbits have some fun too.

The little boy shakes his head. No. I'm not sup-posed to go near them. My father said not to. No, no.

But who'll ever know, we say. We won't tell. Really. Or can your rabbits talk?

No-o-o.

Then what's the problem, we ask in our best, just-want-to-be-your-friend voices.

The little boy bites his thumb.

OK then, see you. Bye-bye. We shrug our shoulders, start to walk off.

Wait, the little boy says panicky. What do you want me to do?

Just open the cages and let those poor rabbits visit.

He shakes his head. Oh no!

Why not?

Because they jump on each other and go like this. He moves his tongue rapidly in and out.

We suppress a giggle. Really? C'mon. We don't believe you. You're making that up.

No, no, that's what they do.

Let's see it. Just for a moment, OK?

Finally the little boy opens locks, pulls up the cage dividers, and a mad scramble ensues. Rabbits bounce around like rubber balls. Their furs are streaks. The little mouse-colored scruffy males are the worst. They pounce from one female Angora rabbit to the next, their energy never waning. Hop-hop-hop.

See? The little boy says, tears in his eyes. I was right. How will I ever get them back into their cages now?

We have tears in our eyes too, from laughing so loud that we're crying. Just wait till they get tired, we say. From the looks of it, that won't be for quite a while.

🐰 🐰 🐰

But this time there are no other kids involved,

thank goodness. I always feel bad later, after we've tricked some poor little kid. But now there's just the three of us so far back in the backyard that we can't be seen through the kitchen window even if Julie were looking. It's just Ger and Rudi running around naked. Apple trees bend at the waist, their long branches touch the top of the grass. They make arches. Tents. The hedges are thick green walls shutting out the outside world. C'mon, let's play, Rudi says. Strip down.

I do. Off with all those stiff clothes. Without soap, all that washing does is make our clothes turn into boards. But now the sun is out, speckling the overgrown meadow through the tree leaves. The world and war are far removed. All our other siblings are gone, and Vati's sorting through the pieces of his best junk in the cellar.

In the farthest corner of our neglected yard, we kids play survivors. We feel like we're the last people on earth and try to out-leap each other from joy. Free, alive, warm, and hungry yes, but that's a constant. Our naked bodies are skinny. Ribs protrude, we have dirt streaks on arms and legs, look like those scruffy wild rabbits the way we bounce through the grass, start rolling on the ground, tussle with each other.

At times our older brothers grab us, throw us on the ground, hop on our chests, pummel us in the face. That game is called "Amis." The beater is the American; the one getting whipped is the German. But now there's no beating, no trying to make someone cry on purpose. It's not the aim of this game to hurt you.

No, this is all in fun. We're deer leaping; pale doves flitting around.

Let's do it, Rudi says.

What? I ask. I just got here and nobody told me the rules yet.

Rudi stands up and thrusts his hip forward. Let's put it in, *Dummkopf*.

I look at him. He has light-blue eyes, his dark blond hair stands up in tufts, his face is red from all the running. Breathing heavily Ger stands beside him with her dark-blue eyes, curly light brown hair that used to be blonde. She's so pretty. She's never had an ugly day. Heda, who's not here now, is startling-looking with clear-brown, intelligent eyes, a beautiful carved face, a graceful body. But when Ger was born all the prettiness of the family was used up. That left none for me. And I'm not quick either, so I don't know what to do.

Fortunately Ger asks, How? Which was what I was going to ask, plus why?

Ger doesn't ask why; she knows why.

Rudy grabs his little thing that has grass on it from rolling on the ground, picks off the blades, starts pumping it up with one hand. The little thing gets red, redder. Quick, he says, steps up to Ger, who opens her legs and he sticks it between them.

Scheisse, he says.

What happened? Me again.

It's not going in. He is angry.

I still don't know what we're playing, but I'm the youngest of us and for once trying not to be a coward. Let me try.

Again Rudi rubs his thing up and down, pumps it fast, then pokes it between my legs where it feels like a limp finger. It just lies between my skinny legs. Press your legs together, dammit, he says.

I do.

Not now. Rudi is getting angrier. He's pumping again. First I have to get it in you.

In me? We try again, but it doesn't get any easier. Even though his pumping makes his little thing red and a tiny bit stiff, by the time he shoves it between my legs and in me, it's always limp again. But we keep trying. How we keep trying. My stomach growls at intervals.

It's just not working, Rudi says in disgust.

What's wrong? Ger wonders.

Maybe it's because we haven't eaten anything, I say. We streak around the yard, inspect the apple trees, one has green fruit, the size of pebbles. We cram half a dozen of those sour balls into our mouths, chew quickly, then try again.

Nothing.

Rudi's arm gets tired. Here, you try it, he says. Ger pumps him, but again the effects last only seconds. The same is true when I try. More apples, more. Still nothing happens even when we lie down on the grass. Rudi takes turns lying on top of Ger and me, and we poke his thing where we think it ought to go. But it just won't go in. It's too floppy.

That night I wake up with the worst bellyache of my life—worse than any hunger pains I ever had. I start crying, first softly, then louder. I know what's wrong. Oh no, no, no. I cry so loud that Julie comes running to my bedside. What's the matter?

I have a terrible stomachache.

What in the world from?

I don't know. I just hurt so bad. I think I'll die.

Oh, don't worry, it'll go away. Try to get some sleep.

I cry louder. I can't stop crying. Please, please, please. Don't get mad.

Why should I get mad with you for having a stomachache?

Because we did something.

What?

Something bad.

By then Ger is sitting up in bed, shaking her head, pressing a finger against her lips. Rudi pokes his head into the room, a look of warning on his face. Shut up, he mouths. I see him, see what Ger is trying to get me to do—clam up. But I can't stop. I'm so scared.

Julie, her voice like a hammer: What...did...you... do...?

We played so much until—Rudi's shaking two fists behind Julie's back. His punches hurt, and I know he'll deliver many of them, but still I'm too scared to stop telling.

Until what?

Until I got pregnant.

What? Slowly Julie digs all the details out of me. Vati comes, yawns, and gives Ger and Rudi a whipping. I would've gotten one too, but I'm in such pain already.

I stay in bed the next day until the diarrhea from all those green apples has passed. With it goes my stomachache. Dammit, kids our age can't get pregnant, Ger says after a day or two when she finally starts speaking to me again. We won't let you play with us next time.

But I didn't know, I say.

Why didn't you just keep your mouth shut, coward?

❦ ❦ ❦

The next weekend after more nonstop hiking, I'm lying on wet grass again with all my brothers, sisters and Vati, waiting for sleep. I'm determined not to be a coward again when I finally manage to corner Vati.

I don't know when that will be, but I want to find out the truth.

What happened with the Jews?

But for now I stew over the fact again that I'm not like the rest of the family. I'm no good, I'm just not as brave. Weakling!

Even nature knows it. Why else would all those bugs and slugs and mosquitoes that the piles of wet grass have attracted always pick on me? They hone in on me, creep in the opening of my shirt. Ticks make my scalp itch. I scrape them off. Their heads remain embedded in my scalp and soon bulge big again. Bugs bite me wherever a piece of my skin is exposed. Centipedes scurry into my underclothes, looking for a nest. Mosquitoes land on my face and bite me through whatever I cover myself with.

The war's over, but no peace.

I have to scratch and scratch; welts spring up everywhere. Oozing sores bring more pests. My sores never heal; my nose is running year-round.

Dried snot is always caked under my nose. My eyes have deep dark circles around them.

Ger has all the prettiness. I have all the ugliness.

When I look in the mirror, I see hollow cheeks, staring eyes, lips that are bitten. Steel-brown hair in dirty wisps. Long bony arms and legs that aren't coordinated. Why didn't Mutti throw me out when I was born?

Now in the dark woods, wild animals make nocturnal sounds. One calls; another answers. Roo-coo? Roo-coo.

I listen to them, feel so alone, abandoned. A misfit.

Why can't I be like the rest of my family?

No answer. It's just like all those questions I have—never an answer.

The tall firs surrounding our clearing, where we're stretched out on a wet patch of grass, are bogeymen that seem to step closer to me every second. So I avert my eyes, but I'm wide awake while the world is asleep. Surrounded by all my snoozing siblings, I ache and ache. It's more than hunger pains, more than "pregnant" pains. It's deep inside.

My father reaches out in sleep, wants to hug me tight, cuddle, kiss me passionately again—

No. No more.

I move away from him and sandwich myself between my eight snoring brothers. Tears trickle down the corners of my eyes, run down my face, mingle with the wetness on the grass.

Why?

As an answer, one of the little boys is peeing on me.

Hope some of those bugs get soaked by the hot stream.

CHAPTER 6

Condom
Ball

T he American soldiers aren't the only conquerors of Bavaria after World War II. There are other troops too. Because of the strategic location of our house, we are invaded again. A contingent of French soldiers bursts into the house, takes over all the rooms, stores mountains of food supplies in Oma's room that has a good lock, and watches every move we make.

A colorful French flag waves out of the same attic window where the American one fluttered just a few months ago.

While the American soldiers, once they secured the village, only kept an eye on Julie when she had to cook their meals, and otherwise lounged in the yard, smoked, chewed pink gum and laughed at us kids, the French soldiers take their war work more seriously.

They search every inch of Diessen for German guerrillas, march along the deserted dirt lanes, occupy the piles of gray rubble and black bomb craters that dot the landscape and are suspicious of all Germans until they've made sure they are unarmed.

This time Vati's at home when the soldiers barge in. Fortunately he speaks French, so he can communicate with the occupation. But his attempts at conversation never get anywhere during the day when the business of war's at hand. The relationship between the occupiers and the occupied is cool from nine and five. Only after official war/hostility hours can the soldiers relax and mingle with us.

That's when they stop working and do target practice in our backyard. I haven't been in the backyard in days, but now I'm back there again. It's later in the year; the yard's swathed in dark green. Apple and pear trees have emerald leaves. The sky is blue and limitless. The wild flowers shimmer in every color combination possible. Scarlet, egg-yolk yellow, periwinkle blue, dark lilac....Since the Amis left us, we've of course been eating flowers and grass again—all we have. But the French soldiers don't care. They squash our flowers, stretch out on their stomachs in the grass, aim at our cherry tree halfway up the trunk and shoot. Then they target other trees. A cheerful rat-tat-tat ensues.

What excitement. My brothers, sisters and I, wearing our droopy rags, barefoot and hungry—all French meals are strictly closed to us kids—streak between the rain of bullets from one side of the yard to the other.

The bullets whiz past us, and I don't know why Vati doesn't stop us. Maybe he's like Julie now, just trying to hang on. But nobody ever makes us stop. So we soar, fly, scurry, back and forth across the yard, while the soldiers pepper tree after tree with bullets. If any of us were to slip, slow down or stumble, we'd get hit.

For the soldiers fire in a precise time sequence.

But we kids have such fun. We know that for the moment the French soldiers don't see us as enemies, but rather as quick little rascals. Or as pop-up figures at a country fair. Bang-bang-bang.

Later they invite us to play sports, be part of their teams. That happens after it gets too dark for the shooting drills. One soldier divides their group into two teams, a rope is strung across the yard, then the teams pick us kids as extra members.

Even I get picked.

One soldier takes a pretty white balloon out of his pocket, blows it up and a fierce volleyball game starts. The shimmering white globe floats over the rope back and forth amid squeals of delight or dismay. A mysterious moon dropped low. The sky is always dim, but light streams out of the house from all the rooms the soldiers have confiscated from us. In the descending darkness, the soldiers are large shapes. We kids smaller shapes that come and go.

The game goes on. French voices are background music.

Other times, the white balloons are filled with water and we play until somebody gets splashed in the face and hurt, but just a little. There are always more balloons. Every soldier has an unending supply and the games make the evenings pass. In the darkness no war has happened. The world is whole if only for an hour.

The soldiers are just young men; we are kids.

Vati can be heard talking with the French colonel. Julie's wringing her hands in the kitchen: There's hardly anything to scrape out of the pots, but she manages to give every child a spoonful.

In the mornings, it's back to serious combat. At times the soldiers yell in outrage, and Vati yells back. Guns are drawn; we're the enemy again. The losers. The beaten.

We kids have to line up in the yard and empty our pockets. It seems during the previous evening some of the French food was stolen. Again. An interrogation gets underway. The soldiers call out questions and my father translates.

Heda, did you go into the soldiers' supply room last night?

She twists her braids, chews the ends. No, I didn't.

Did you take some of their food?

Her thin face is defiant. No, I didn't.

My father's expression is painful as if he wishes he didn't have to take part in this court martial, but he has to go on translating for the French soldiers: They had 142 cans of cheese, now it's only 141.

Hansi is next. The same questions rain.

I don't know anything about it, he says. Didn't do it.

Then comes Heini, next in age.

He denies any knowledge of the missing cheese. I was out in the yard all evening playing.

But somebody got the key and sneaked into their room, Vati translates.

Well, that wasn't me. Wasn't me. Wasn't me. Under their breaths the brothers add, dammit! Shit.

On down the line it goes. All kids are interrogated at this military tribunal. Serious expressions everywhere, hands waving, voices rising. Vati looks ever more embarrassed.

There's no pause until they come to Ger. Her blue eyes light up. Ringlets dance on her head and surround a face copied from the golden cherubim and seraphim angels floating on the ceiling in the big Catholic church in Diessen.

Not only that, she is an angel. Of all the children she's the most obedient, the best behaved, the cutest. Whenever Julie has a breakdown and all the housework is left for us girls, Heda manages to absent herself immediately. Must be a talent learned from Vati, but all kinds of relatives feel sorry for Heda being the eldest of our clan.

So someone always invites her.

That means that Ger and I are left with all the housework, but Ger never complains. Her mending is a masterpiece, her scrubbed pots sparkle. She's sweet to everyone, saves crumbs for starving animals. She does a few chores brilliantly; I do everything else just as quick and sloppy as I can. I always just want to get to the end of the never-ending chores and be free for a moment. Catch my breath just once.

Be a child for just one hour. Just one time.

Not Ger. She's just nicer than I am. And better. Prettier. Braver.

This day, Ger smiles as the questioning gets to her. Curtsies, bows. But the French soldiers wave

Vati on. *Non, non.* Don't waste time with her. The Colonel winks at Ger: We know she's innocent. This little doll had no part in the crime, the outrageous thievery.

Ger curtsies again, throws a kiss, steps away. The interrogation goes on. Next is Rudi, just as defiant as the other boys. Then it's on to me. I have no idea what happened to the cheese, I say. Only wish I had, I think.

On the questions go, down to Paul and to Joachim...on and on. Then the punishment—all of us, except Ger, receive a whipping for stealing and for lying about it. Vati carries out the punishment. We kids let the slaps pelt us like a hail storm. Big deal.

Afterwards, the older boys look angry enough to explode.

Of course they've been beaten before many times, but to get a beating for something they haven't done in view of everybody, including the soldiers, hurts. Even after the court-martial, the boys keep hissing all kinds of threats.

Damn those French idiots. Damn Vati!

Ger calms them down by sharing her fine cheeses with them. Brie, camembert. She's the one who sneaked into the store room. The boys cram wedges into their mouths between more threats. They only stop while they chew to snap at me.

Can't *you* make yourself useful for once?

Why don't you steal a gun from those French *Arschloecher*? Fool, coward.

CHAPTER 7

Rosary Reel

I can't get hold of a gun; not even a sharp knife. Not tough enough. But I spend all day trying to figure out a way to scrape up something edible. Problem is, the French occupation forces leave us too like the Amis. And with them goes our last chance of stealing some food regularly.

On the way out of town, the first jeep in the French convoy stops. The soldiers are looking for a souvenir. There's nothing now. Everything valuable has already been liberated by the GIs. *Mon Dieu*. It's tough to be the second wave of occupation. Even the churches look bare now. The priests, nuns and monks have buried their valuables in hidden crypts. While they hand over food at gunpoint, they're not about to part with any religious relics.

So what souvenirs can the French soldiers scoop up? The driver of the lead vehicle gets out, picks me out from all the barefoot kids with running noses that chase alongside the jeeps and trucks waving, plunks me on the lap of the officer sitting next to him.

The officer smiles. Well done. Our own little scarecrow, our war victim.

Then the caravan pulls out.

And I feel my face cracking. I must be smiling: *Wunderbar.* I get to ride in a French jeep, Me-me-me. I'm the one. Not Ger, Heda or any of my brothers. I was picked out, sit high off the ground in a real jeep. I look back and wave at the other kids. My face is still contorting. It's an odd feeling, just like the time the nuns in school singled me out. We have few books, so every day Sister Gertrud reads a short paragraph for us to write. It's always a few sentences by a famous author: Goethe, Schiller, Mark Twain, Shakespeare....

After we try laboriously to write down what Sister reads, she pulls back a gray sheet from the broken chalkboard on which the paragraph holds forth in big letters. Then it's our job to copy all the words we misspelled 20 times. But last week Sister dictated a paragraph that sounded familiar. When she announced the author, my face burned.

Not from embarrassment but from pride. That day's paragraph was one I had written and turned in for homework the week before. All the other kids had to write *my* paragraph.

Mine.

Now sitting on the lap of the French officer and riding in the jeep, I feel the same way. And the mask of my face has broken to pieces. I feel flushed and yet proud. Finally something good is happening.

The caravan picks up speed; Diessen lies far

behind us now. The tall church steeples wink when I crane my head. The bright red roofs are little daubs of paint far in the distance. White walls make the town look new. So many houses have been fixed up again. Slowly Bavaria is repairing itself. Up on the hill, our house isn't visible, wrapped in its many coats of green.

The French soldiers talk. The same musical tones that have floated through our house during the French occupation swirl around my head like colorful ribbons. My officer holds me tight on his lap. I don't understand a word of what he's talking about but know he won't abandon me out here on the dusty country street that winds south toward the Alps. The military caravan follows the curving roads. The trees lining them are missing bark, where other starving families picked at them.

But small new saplings are beginning to sprout.

I feel my officer's arms closing around me. His voice is a cozy cape, his warm breath on the back of my neck is a scarf soft like Mutti's old slip. All I have to do is lean back, think of my good luck, stay on this nice man's lap, never ever go back home again to the ice house.

The screaming, starving. Getting punched by the never-ending brothers. The filth, worms. The craziness….

No more being a slave.

No more having to be ashamed all the time because of Dachau.

I'm safe now. The war's finally over for me. I managed to escape. The shame I always feel about being poor, being German, being one of Vati's horde of children is going, going—gone....

But won't they miss me? My sisters? All those big boisterous brothers?

What will Julie do without me? And what about the little brothers? Who's going to make sure they get at least one meal when Julie's in the hospital again?

Ha, that's not for me to worry about anymore. I'm just a little girl and will always have something to eat from now on. Won't freeze anymore in winter. Maybe in France I'll get something to wear that's not ragged. I'll get some nice words, like that soft good-smelling breath bathing my neck.

But what about Vati and those questions I have?

In France I'll become French. I'll never get to the bottom of what went on. I'll never know what *really* happened.

Halt, I say, stop. I don't want to go back, really don't want to. But know I must go home. It's that guilty feeling I always get when I've done something wrong; it's crowding me again. The Catholic nuns call it conscience, the priest, sin.

Whatever it is—all I know I have to get back to our house. Now.

Halt, I say louder. Halt!

The officer gives a sigh, kisses me, hugs me tight, I feel the tip of his tongue on my neck. Just close your eyes, I tell myself, sink back against his chest, feel his strong arms around me. He smells so good. Don't be a coward again. Tell the French soldiers to go on. Drive.

But I am a coward, a weakling. The convoy grinds

to a halt, I hop off, run barefoot back all the way to Diessen. Such a long, hot dusty way. Five, six kilometers. I get to our road red-faced and breathless. I race up the hill, never mind that I'm stubbing my toes. I scold myself every step for ever having considered leaving my family.

I was bad to even think of going with those soldiers. Becoming a French girl; living someone else's life.

By now everyone will be wondering what happened to me. So worried about me—where, oh where is our Eri?

I have to gulp for breath when I fling myself through the trees and bushes in our yard to get back to the old house. The yard is so still. They must all be down at the town square trying to find a way to chase after the caravan. Stop it. Vati will knock the French officer down, snatch me away, carry me home....

I am what keeps the family going. The middle child—five older kids, five younger ones, once they're all born....

But no one's been looking for me. My siblings don't even look up when I return. I wander through the deserted house whose rooms are dark and barren now. Only old metal bedsteads, unsellable on the black market, remain, and a few dirty mattresses with overlapping stains and shrouded with torn and filthy sheets. A pile of ragged blankets cowers on the floor.

The kitchen looks most forbidding. The stove is icy. Warm water takes just so long before it gets unsatisfying as a drink, so we drink it cold. Besides, firewood is scarce and has to be saved for the slight chance that some day something can be found again to cook.

So yes. It's all back to before we were occupied, except it's worse now. Licking out the delicious Ami plates, then stealing from the French gave us hope.

Now all we have is our hunger. It hits us worse after we've had real food. But we do have water to drink. That makes our stomachs distend, taut like those blown-up French condoms we used to play with.

A few times we find some wheat still growing in a field, which we tear out and take home to mash with a hammer before picking out the hard husks. But our diseased, loose teeth make it hard for us to chew wheat kernels. But we try. On special days we manage to find some rotten turnips in a field or steal some from a neighbor. Sometimes even a few shriveled potatoes. Then we get a little bite of potato bread. That's a delicious mush made of coarse flour mixed with grated raw potatoes and baked in a pan. Mmm, is it ever so scrumptious.

What's incredible is sitting in the sun in the afternoon and gnawing on a hunk of potato bread knowing the big boys are not at home. So they can't grab it away from me. Slap me if I whine. And the little boys are sleeping. So they can't toddle out and stand in front of me, their eyes wide and begging, their drenched diaper rags down on their knees and stinking, their little fanny cheeks crisscrossed with pus-filled sores.

So I'm in heaven with my very own hunk of bread! Mine, all mine. Slowly I try to nibble at it, make the bread last forever. But my gnawing hunger pains demand bigger bites. More and more. So I take bigger bites, sling large chunks down. Who knows where danger lurks?

But chewing something edible is the best part of our lives. People's jaws get restless when they never get a chance to chew. It's the physical act of moving one's jaws and tongue. It's satisfying, and the taste of the potatoes—that is, swallowing something better than grass—is heaven.

Oh, to have something other than water filling our stomachs. And then once a week or every other week to actually have an occasion to go to the bathroom, not just pee outside. That's miraculous. There's no paper to wipe with, of course. But we still have a few old books. So you tear out a few pages that are slick, hard, treacherous. But if you crinkle up the glossy pages, work them into a ball, smooth them out, scrunch them again, then flatten them once more, you're finally able to make them soft enough not to hurt your backside permanently.

Often we have a few sheets of paper prepared but no reason for using them. Digestion stops when no food comes in. Of course, the bushes have leaves, so we're all right outside. Leaves are much softer, but you never bring leaves inside. Inside it's only paper. An unwritten law. Besides, what would our guests think?

We have to save the best "toilet paper" for them.

Must never forget who we are, where we come from. The family history, our place in society, the long line of famous Vierlings. That's why Vati gets furious when the little boys start to go begging from house to house. Under no circumstances, he yells, it's just not done. What will people think? The Vierlings don't go begging!

We starve in private.

Better a funeral than let other people know how poor we are.

But really. What does he expect us to do? He has an old toothbrush he chews on to keep his hunger pains at bay, and he's grown up. Same goes for Julie. She can always look forward to some meals at the mental hospital. But hey, what about us kids?

We're just plain hungry.

Problem is, there's nobody to steal from anymore, not a soul. People have gotten so careful about their own measly food supplies. Windows are barred; big locks installed. Some people take whatever small amounts of flour and rice they have left to bed with them. So even the cleverest kids among us come home empty-handed from our forays into town.

It's frustrating to spend all day trying to steal something and come home with zilch.

But what about all those other small villages we pass on our forced hikes?

No one knows us there, Vati. Can't we go and beg there? Please? Please? Please?

By then he's too starved himself to object. Sure, go ahead. Just don't tell them who you are.

Yippee! The three of us, Ger, Rudi and I, don't have to do much to get ready. We tear our rags a little more, smear mud on ourselves and into our matted hair, practice grinning to show our loose trench-mouth teeth. They are rotting so nicely at the gum line.

But Rudi isn't satisfied with how our teeth look

and paints them black all the way, making us look worse. He laughs his infectious laugh as he adds some extras. Sticks big dead bugs in our hair, picks off the scabs from our never-healing wounds to make them ooze. Rakes a nail up and down our legs. Don't blow your nose, he says to me, a wasted comment. What do I have to blow my nose with, except my forearms already smeared with snot?

But we're excited about the adventure. Finally we're allowed to go begging, like all other poor kids we see so often. What fun. On the way to the first village we practice. Ger can cry bitterly on command. What a talented actress. The pitiful, bedraggled way she looks is enough to melt a heart of stone. A begging beauty; she'll go first.

I'm not bad myself with all my running sores, yellow-green snot dangling down to my chin and my spindly legs. The circles under my eyes are black as shoe polish. I itch everywhere and scratch. My welts are huge, but Ger's skin is too unmarred. So Rudi dabs "gashes" on with red paint. And using dirty rags, he bandages his feet so it looks like he was wounded after stepping on a landmine and can only hobble with great difficulty.

But there's a problem. Rudi forgets about his injuries, and he has a tendency to break into uproarious laughter when he sees us sobbing on command. He starts bouncing around like crazy. And he laughs again when we hide our hole-filled shoes and walk barefoot down a lane. For effect, he hobbles grotesquely and shoves us into cow dung. But finally he realizes it's serious. Show time. He keeps himself under perfect control when we knock on the first farmhouse. A chubby, middle-aged woman opens the door, her face deep-lined.

Please, oh please give us something to eat, Ger cries. Please.

Where are you from? she asks.

Oh, from far, far. So far. We're war orphans, I sob bitterly. We have nobody. Nothing—

Haven't eaten in a whole year, Rudi adds. That's overdoing it and he knows it but keeps looking pitiful. I don't know how he does it.

The woman sniffs, shakes her head in sympathy as she steps back. *Ach Gott*, you poor, poor things. She asks us inside where it smells so good I fill my lungs to capacity with the aroma. That alone is worth the 10-kilometer hike and stepping into the cow dung that's now caked between my toes.

Wiping her hands on her apron, the woman points to a corner where a kneeling bench crouches in front of a small altar adorned with blue-gold icons and fake-blood-dripping crucifixes. She drapes a clean towel over the upholstered pew. Go over there and pray. Pray hard, she says. One thing I don't have and that's food for heathens, understand?

Oh, don't worry, we're good little Catholics, Ger says, batting her eyes.

Then go on, start saying the rosary, the woman says. Right now....

Panic hits us. We've rehearsed the begging so very well, have the pitiful looks down and the injured walk, but haven't practiced any rosaries. Of course, we know some prayers. Julie always insists we go to church, so we know the routine.

Can we pray the way we always pray? Ger asks.

The woman nods.

Our Father, we begin because that's the first thing that comes to mind, and squeeze onto the bench. Thou art in heaven—then silence. What in the world comes next? My mind is a blank—the delicious aroma has blanketed out everything. Ger and Rudi are in the same shape. We don't remember what comes next. Oh, we're in deep trouble now, but we're so excited. This is the performance of our lifetime. Yet we'll flop for sure unless we remember the rest of this prayer. Our Father, Thou art in heaven…?

We start over, but don't get beyond that, even when we try a third time. Our Father, Thou art in heaven and…? and…? and…?

This is desperately serious, yet Rudi starts smirking. Suddenly he realizes his bandages have come off. Later he blames it all on me. Says it's the way my dangling snot washed the black color off my teeth, so they're almost normal-looking again. And we are shedding dead bugs on the floor left and right. Ger's bloody gashes are also fading fast before our eyes.

Fortunately at that point the woman goes down the basement and we really pour it on. We start wailing, throw around all kinds of gibberish interspersed with *Lieber Gott im Himmel* and *Helf uns, Strahlender Engel*. We make up prayers nobody's heard of, recite whatever religious phrases come to our minds over and over. Call on all the saints we ever heard of—hallelujah, hallelujah, hallelujah, holy Saint*s Butterbrot* and *Marmalade*—until we hear her steps recede.

Then we go crazy. Catapult up and strut from joy. This poor woman believes us. She thinks we're good little Christian beggars. Fooled her, didn't we? We're beggars all right, but we aren't good Christians! I find it hard to believe in a Jesus who lets innocent Jews die.

So we burst out laughing. Whirl around the pew in circles, slap hands together, scream, throw curse words around just like we did moments before all those saints' names. We shake our fannies, make ugly noises. Do cartwheels around the kneeling bench. Make evil gestures, spit. Count off each sacrilegious circle as a set of prayers. Sure is fun.

Until the very moment when we hear the woman climb up the basement stairs again, we dance our pagan reel, then kneel quickly down on the bench again. Such meek little lambs we become again. Oh, we poor innocent little orphans. With our heads hanging and eyes shut and as pious an expression on our faces as we can muster, we murmur amen, amen.

Over and over. Amen.

Good children, the woman says, very good children. She hands each of us some apples along with the most incredible gift we've ever received—a warm *semmel*. Oh, oh, how the praying paid off. The saints saved us, or the cursing, or the savage dancing. We don't know which, but thank you, thank you. We'll go to church every day from now on. Maybe....But oh, what a wonderful incredible present this is—a little freshly baked roll. So perfect it's a shame to eat it. It's the most beautiful thing in the universe. A wonder of the world. Actual flour dough has gone into that roll—and not one slice of potato.

We thank the woman again with many curtsies and amens! Declare her a true saint, vow to name our children after her.

My name's Agnes, she says blushing.

We'll remember that, sure, forever, we chorus. Back out of the farm, scraping and bowing, all of us now hobbling in elated confusion. We forgot who was hurt by the land mine. Snot bubbles out of all our noses. We run screaming from laughter down the road away from the farmhouse, we dance the rude rosary dance again, swallow the apples, worms, seeds, stems and all, then caress our treasures, our darling little rolls. Sniff them, rub them like pets, lick them like candy, taste a crumb. Finally we can't stand it any longer. We devour them in two, three bites. Oh heaven. It's the best food we've ever eaten.

Then we dance again, a crazy drunken dirty dance, we make animal noises, collapse on the ground intertwined—three dirty kids, ages seven, seven and a half, and eight.

We feel stuffed for the first time in years. Where there's usually a hollow in our stomachs, there's now a hill. We are proud, stick it out.

Oh, oh, how wonderful life is.

We solved the food shortage.

When we see a dried dog turd, we kick it like a football. Name it Agnes.

But how good it feels to have this skill: We know how to beg and beg good. There are so many other farmhouses. Bavaria's filled with them. Oh, oh. All we need is to go home and memorize some prayers. Damn. Brush up on some bible passages too. Study some saints. Be able to reel off rosaries in our sleep.

Who knows what we can extort from those simple farm women next? If we'd prayed harder, longer, more fervently, we might have gotten two semmels each. Maybe three. Stuff our tummies. So much happiness....

If only Mutti could see us now.

If only Mutti hadn't died.

CHAPTER 8

Holy Theft

Too bad word gets out soon about that family with the swarm of wild kids who specialize in begging and conning nice farm women. From then on, doors slam into our faces. The simple-minded fat farm *Frauen* become tigresses and charge at us, hefting rolling pins like clubs. We hobble for real now because not wanting to come home empty-handed we've walked farther afield, decided not to wear any shoes at all and in the course of those long fruitless wanderings cut our heels, stump toes and scratch our soles enough to make us limp. All cuts turn angry red, fester for months. That takes all the fun out of begging. Those folks call themselves Christians? Won't even give us a bite? Made us memorize all those dumb prayers for nothing?

What's the matter with them?

Naturally we're not allowed to hit up the people in town, some of whom soon sprout stomachs again.

Their cheeks fill out from feasting on *Knoedel* and *Schweinsbraten*. It's that old double standard again. Just because we are who we are, we have to suffer in secret. Disguise our despair. Other poor kids are so lucky. They get to flaunt their poverty. But not us.

For us it's something shameful. Something to hide.

Yet no matter how much we pretend to have plenty, Vati's desperate again like he was before he married Julie. He wants to bury himself in the cellar, in a small cell paneled with metal bits, and invent. Invent, invent. His brilliant mind is exploding with new ideas. But he's constantly being disturbed by all these dirty, hungry kids, some of whom refuse to knuckle down. Refuse to starve in silence. The hungrier the older boys get, the more they become a pack of wolves, roam the house and yard, snatch away anything edible a younger child has managed to find, to save, to linger over. Slap-slap-slap. The sporadic outbursts of crying denote the pack's meandering.

Vati decides that wholesale thieving will do the trick. Aren't the wheat fields of the Dominican Order, which spread like plush golden carpets on the outskirts of Diessen, too vast to be watched on all sides?

Well, let's find out. Let's go.

He lines us kids up at five in the morning, gives us empty sacks and leads us away from the house to a spot that's hidden from view. Go to it. If you get caught, run like the devil. Your last name is Schmitt, understand? You live on the other side of the lake. Got it?

We nod. With kitchen knives we hack away at the tall stalks of wet wheat, make a mess, rip out what we can't cut. The sun's about to come up and there's no one around, but the stalks are tough. Yanking them out of the ground cuts into our skin. Our hands look like they've been lashed with a whip when we come home exhausted a couple of hours later and throw whole sheaves on the kitchen floor. Plunk down at the table, eagerly wait for breakfast.

Instead of being delighted, Julie screams. How am I supposed to turn all those green stalks of wheat that aren't ready for harvest into bread? I'm not Jesus Christ.

You run to church often enough, dammit, Vati says. *Kreuz-Kruzifix-Halleluja!* Cursing he emerges from his lair, pencil and slide rule in hand. Hair, prematurely white, standing up. His eyes have trouble focusing on us. Just now he was *this* close to a scientific breakthrough. So what else could you possibly want? he yells at Julie. Oh, how he resents all these annoying interruptions in his important work. Damn! If it's not one thing, it's another. *Scheisse!* Do I have to do everything around here?

Vati, please, Heda says. She's the eldest after all. Can't we steal something besides this shit?

He sighs. Sighs. The next morning he wakes us at 4 AM. We get up shivering in the cold dark house. Line up as always, tallest to shortest.

Listen, *Kinder.* This isn't for anyone who's scared, he says. Understand? Or for anyone who will make a sound. No *Flaschen* (wimps) today. No *Feigling*s. The other kids stare at me. I shrug, but nobody says anything. We just shiver more in our collection of rags. Our silence reassures him.

Single file, he leads us through the backyard to a tall forbidding hedge. Parting the hedge we see a six-foot fence of barbed wire, a wall of porcupine spikes.

Remember, not one damn sound. I don't care how much it hurts. Try to bleed as little as possible.

Vati climbs the hedge and the barbwire fence quickly like an experienced alpine climber. Easy: He has shoes on, soled by himself with patched rubber pieces. We're all barefoot.

The hedge is no problem. We scale it like martens. But how do you get over that high barbwire? While we're trying to figure that out, Vati whistles.

He's invented a musical message system. Various combinations of notes mean different words. One of these days when one of you kids gets detained by the law and stuck in a cell, I'll walk past the jail house and send you a message, you understand, he explains, not realizing that he's the one who'll end up in police custody.

Now he whistles something simple—two church bell tones, copied from the song of the wood thrushes. It means: C'mon, all clear.

Other, more jarring combinations of notes mean other things like watch out, stop or danger.

But no danger now, only those two drawn-out wood thrush tones again. Crystal clear they hang in the dawn slowly creeping up. C'mon over the fence; all clear.

By then we figured it out. Let's wrap our sweaters, jackets, skirts and pants over all the sharp wire-pieces. Luckily we wear so many clothes. We take off several layers and still have on underclothes. But it takes time to defang those barbs by swathing them. They are not to be denied. Yet in the end stepping on them feels only like stepping on thumb tacks. A few drops of blood are left behind each time one of us kids struggles across the fence, sure, but we make it across, all of us, just as the first rays of sun inch up.

Then we look around and are overcome by awe. Not far in the distance stretches a big, lush, hidden garden we never knew existed. It's the inner sanctum of the nuns. The priests' personal pantry. Created and seen to with infinite care, this peaceful Eden has never been raided by anyone. Even our beloved Amis failed to find it.

But Vati did. So all his long hikes in nature were good for something!

Oh. Oh. What joy it is to see chubby red tomatoes bending their vines almost to the ground. Polished cucumbers the size of our thighs nestle amid great big leaves. Carrots so big the earth has split to make room emerge from the rich brown soil, their green fronds stirring in the breeze. Cabbage heads, bigger than our own, perch proudly on thick stalks and try to outdo one another in size in all their dew-covered beauty.

And over there are nature's rubies: Strawberries the size of baby fists shimmer in luxurious rows. Raspberries preen in the early sun as they cascade from bushes. Gooseberries bigger than eggs look freshly laid amid greenery. And immense patches of blueberries are blankets of sapphire against green velvet.

For us, Vati's thrush-song whistle has a lovely new meaning now:

Pay dirt. Paradise. Go to it!

We love him for showing us paradise. Want to fling ourselves on this bounty, gorge ourselves like ticks. Eat so much we'll get good and sick. And stay sick. We've been sick from hunger many times. Won't it be great to get sick from overeating? Just once? Not to worry, we'll make it back over the fence and home again, if it kills us.

But no, wait. Vati leads us to a thick stand of ancient walnut trees, points at us and at various trees until each one of us nods, takes off, and hides behind a wide trunk. We dance from foot to foot, unable to stand the wait any longer until we see what he's seen. A procession of giant nuns with rakes, shovels and hoes over their shoulders is marching toward Eden. A whole army of the strongest holy women we've ever seen.

Amazons. And at the same time, more nuns whom we didn't notice until now step out of the bushes behind some asparagus beds, their crop-green fingertips reaching for the sky, and move away, chains rattling from their belts—the night shift. No wonder nothing's ever been stolen here. This garden is guarded day and night.

Verdammt! How will we ever get hold of a single rhubarb stalk from those healthy plants over there that beckon us, come get me?

Vati motions—not a sound. We remain frozen behind our walnut trunks, wait and watch until the tired nuns have dragged off and their replacements take over. The new nuns start raking, pulling weeds, picking off dry leaves, set down baskets to be used for their harvest. We die watching them from hunger and from yearning.

A bell chimes. Crystal tones.

All work stops and the nuns move in a circle, heads are bowed. They are praying, maybe for a good crop, continued bounty. Maybe for the poor folks in town.

Maybe for us heathens next door.

The hum of their voices is background music.

Vati is the conductor, starts directing the main orchestra. He points to Heda, holds up two fingers, indicates the tomatoes. She's so fearless, like always. Gets down, weasels her way through the tall grass, hardly visible except for the slight movement of the blades. At the edge of the garden she comes up into a crouch, catches her breath, darts to the tomato plants. Yanks here, there. The blades of grass tremble again and she's back, tomatoes in hand, lifts them to her mouth—

No, Vati indicates. Don't. This is for all of us.

Of course. Indignation washes over her face, yet obediently she lays the tomatoes down. She was only sniffing the red globes, drinking in the bounty.

The nuns keep praying, unaware of what's going on. Please, please, let them keep it up, I pray, relieved to hear the humming drone on. And on.

Vati points to Hansi, quick, the cucumbers, and holds up three fingers. Hansi takes off like a shot fired low to the ground. Grabs the cucumbers still on the run, stuffs them in his pants. On the way back to our stand of trees, he has to slide to make it back to safety. The nuns' religious duties are over for the moment. They stop praying, go back to their gardening. The nuns in charge of the tomatoes and cucumbers look around in alarm. What's happened? They seem astonished. Has a deer or rabbit sneaked up and helped itself, they seem to wonder. They look around some more, trying to detect a sign of whatever animals dared to go after their prize vegetables.

Behind our trees we're trembling, afraid they'll notice the bent grass blades. Discover tracks, advance toward our hiding places. Beat the *Scheisse* out of us with their rakes. We're no match for three dozen Olympic-sized nuns with hoes whose blades sparkle in the sun.

Sure, Vati will take flight, he's uncatchable. Heda and the older boys too, but what about the rest of us?

But luckily so far, the nuns haven't noticed anything amiss. They just shake their heads, go back to their weeding, raking, trying to tie plants to stakes. They loosen the earth, pick dead leaves and bugs off. Tend to their masterpieces.

Eden is silent again. All we can hear is the desperate grumbling of our stomachs, but that's not loud enough to give us away.

At the next prayer session, Vati's more cautious, holds up only one finger as he directs Heini toward the quilt of cabbages. Heini takes off, and in no time streaks back daringly upright, a cabbage tucked tight in his arm, legs moving fast. A football player scoring a touchdown.

Ger is next. While we were waiting she's woven leafy weeds into a covering to camouflage herself. As she advances toward the garden, she looks like a pile of leaves the wind lifts at one place and deposits on another. The pile of leaves returns successfully with a few carrots, while Rudi's already pacing, excited by this game and making plans. He's been looking around, trying to find something, maybe a sharp rock to cut the rhubarb with.

How else can he slice off some of those giant stalks without making noise? We know the stalks are tough. We also love rhubarb pie. And we could kill for some of that asparagus.

At the proper time Rudi starts creeping through the tall grass. It's disappointing to watch him. There's no mad dash to the vegetable beds, no mooning of the oblivious nuns. In the past, Rudi's always been filled with the most mischief. Not now. He just proceeds with utter caution toward his assignment, inches maddeningly slowly toward the holy vegetables, bites off some rhubarb and a few asparagus spears. Not like he would usually, with a big lusty bite, but only with nibbles.

Then he's our Rudi again. True Rudi. From his pocket he produces a handful of pungent dark-brown pellets. Aha, that's what he was looking for earlier. Deer and rabbit dung. We almost clap out loud as we watch him decorate the vegetable beds he raided with a few nice pellets here and there. He's an artist, the way he strategically places the stinking pebbles.

There! That ought to convince those nuns.

Then he's back, hair bristling, eyes shining.

Later on my successful foray to steal strawberries and the little brothers' brave snatching of gooseberries and blueberries are uneventful aftermaths, hardly worth mentioning.

But for days afterwards, we laugh over the shrieks of the nuns when they find the "evidence" of wild animals in their garden, run to get bales of netting that they frantically string up, discuss what kinds of poisonous substances they should lay out overnight....

Say extra prayers over this abomination.

They get so wrapped up in their plans to ensure no more animals will eat the fruits of their sacred labor, that we manage to steal a couple of their baskets. Pile in our goodies, make it back to the wire fence and the hedge without getting caught.

Rudi isn't the only hero that day though. Hansi is one too. Some time during the course of that day, he gets stung by a swarm of bees and not just anywhere, like on the foot or the arm, which happens to us all the time.

We can always tell when spring is coming. It's when we get our first bee stings.

But Hansi gets stung on the face, on his eyelid, of all places. He's allergic to bees. His face swells grotesquely. As a result he can only open one eye and that just a crack. His face is dark red. He has trouble breathing. Tear after tear squeezes from his shut eye, grows into fat drops.

Runs down his thin face, leaving clean trails on his dirty cheeks. Makes him look like an Indian with war paint who's being tortured. Intense pain, sure, but Hansi is the most stoic of all of us. Never makes a sound.

A young man of iron.

CHAPTER 9

Snail Oil

But how often can you raid Eden? Once or twice. Maybe three times if you're very, very careful. Then you get caught. Especially now that the nuns have started letting dogs roam the perimeter of their vegetable fields, big mean scrawny ones, hungry for blood—slaughterhouse dogs. The nuns and the farmers have banded together against us. The nuns have God on their side; the farmers, their pitchforks.

What do we have besides worms, bloated bellies, pus-filled sores, gums with ulcers and rotting teeth?

Nothing. So it's back to stealing that old wheat, which fortunately has ripened. Now Julie's glad to see it come in regularly, and we learn to grind it on flat stones in the backyard. But how can you make something edible out of that dirty home-ground flour without having something resembling lard to fry the flour-water mixture with? Pour coarse flour and water into an ungreased metal dish, bake it in the oven and all you get is a white brick, that's stuck to the sides of the pan.

You have to chip it out. Waste a lot of good food that way.

Then you pure gag on it. And gag on it.

So we need some grease.

But it's so tough to come up with any after the war. We use the wax paper in which margarine comes wrapped up, when we can find some in other people's trash. But those minute residues of fat are soon gone. Then we lick the wax paper, chew it, swallow it. But we still don't have the grease we need. If we only had something valuable left to trade for some. But by now our house is almost bare. The only thing we have too much of is hungry kids, and nobody wants them.

Nobody wants our old mattresses either, peed-on and vomit-stained as they are on both sides, many times over.

So back to the trash piles. We're in luck, find rotten rugs with moth holes so big we can look through. We brush them off. Comb out the fringes and touch them up with paint. Roll the rugs up cleverly so none of the holes are visible, and "sell" them on the black market for a tablespoonful of butter.

These days butter is more valuable than gold.

Then we crouch behind the rubble piles from bombed-out houses and wait. Just wait, until the black marketers unroll the "priceless Persian rugs" we stuck them with, discover the big holes, curse and toss out the rugs again. We wait some more, until the cursing men move on to another village where they set up shop again. By then we have snatched our good rugs back, go through the same process, roll them up into another enticing bundle and "sell" them again for another dab of butter or a spoonful of rancid oil.

A tiny pat of margarine. Whatever we can get.

But even that good deal stops working. Sooner or later the same black marketeers show up. And this time they're armed. So the carpet business is all over with, and still we need lard desperately. Whatever we've gotten so far has long been used up.

But never mind now. Vati has another brilliant idea, always does. It's a very wet summer, which brings out snails all over Bavaria. You can hardly take a step and not see one.

So early one morning, Vati wakes us, gives us each a bucket or an empty can, and sends us out of the house. Pick up all the snails in town.

Hurry, not a moment to waste. Don't let anyone else get them.

Soon huge piles of snails squirm on our kitchen floor. Most try to escape and crawl everywhere. Others, finding themselves in strange surroundings, are overcome by a mating frenzy and cling to each other, resulting in giant clumps of snails. The clumps glom on to other giant moving masses until the kitchen floor, walls, and ceiling sprout large ugly cancers that never stop moving, never stop forming new giant undulating configurations. On the floor and everywhere else slimy trails run like snot from a giant's nose. Sucking sounds erupt when we try to separate the clumps.

Vati is thrilled with the sight. No more black market ever, he says. Hallelujah. No more begging, no more being poor.

Why not, we ask.

Can't you see, he says, pointing to the giant snot trails.

We see the big damn mess.

This is how we're going to cash in, he says. Finally. We're going to be rich. Your mother can buy whatever she wants.

But there's nothing to buy. Heda.

Scheisse. For enough damn money, you can buy anything on earth. Julie can finally stop all that screeching. No more of her damn nervous breakdowns either, don't you understand?

His words are rain on parched earth. Smiles appear like desert flowers on our filthy faces. We start dancing, weave our way through the mountains of coupling snails. Vati is the smartest man in town, maybe in all of Bavaria. In the whole country.

You bet. And he's never said we'd be rich before until just now, right? So he has a good reason, sure. All those endless hours in his cellar room finally paid off. He's not breeding Angora rabbits, hasn't yet finished the first electric car—his best invention so far—but he's on to something new that's great. That's even better. *Ach du lieber!* We can feel it in our bones.

This is our day. Hope is as tangible as this roiling snail mess.

How are we going to get rich? I ask, even though I get a kick in the shins from somebody. The bubble of joy is too wonderful to be pierced by one of my stupid questions.

Who cares how? Didn't you hear what Vati said? Ger fusses me out.

But I don't understand—

Just watch, Vati cuts me off. He gets out the one kitchen appliance, a huge meat grinder, that Julie has been hiding. Of all her wonderful modern gadgets and possessions that she brought into the family and held on to, this is the last one. She's been saving it to trade for a spoonful of sugar, a drop of milk, something extra special for when she's really at the end of her rope.

Vati screws the meat grinder to the kitchen table. Now watch this. With both hands he scoops up some wriggling snails, stuffs them into the wide metal mouth. Now crank that thing, crank it hard, he says, beaming at the boys who for once can't wait to help with a kitchen chore. We're going to be rich!

The older boys turn the handle and grind the squirming snails down while the younger kids are waiting eagerly.

What's in those snails? Gold? *Mensch*, am I curious.

Shut your mouth, will you! My siblings treat me as if my asking would make the miracle disappear, whatever it will be. But I shut up, push through the little boys who, plates in hand, are already waiting by the snail encrusted cold stove for something delicious to squeeze out of the ground-up snails.

I can already see what that is—disgusting gray-green juice.

But Vati's getting more excited. More snails, more snails. C'mon.

The boys heap them together, lift them up with

their plates, rush massive piles of them to the meat grinder. Squish them down into the opening, put their hands on top of Hansi's, who is still manning the handle, and help him turn it.

Grind-grind-grind. A family enterprise.

Just another minute, Vati says, then it will all come out. And then we can sell it. Get rich quick. No more starving ever.

I have to ask: What will come out?

Open your eyes, won't you? The damn fat from all those snails. Vati's smiling. C'mon, kids, hurry up. Move that crank harder, faster.

We're only too glad to believe him, our Vati, our white-haired emperor, who towers over the tidal waves of snails. The smartest man we know. Who can do anything, can make miracles happen. His voice rises:

Somebody wash out those cans. Clean those buckets, hop to it. We need them for all that the grease we're producing. All that oil we're making. We'll sell it all, make all kinds of cash.

Ger and Heda start rinsing out every container they can get their hands on. Some snails latch onto them, crawl up their backs. They keep on working feverishly. I peel the snails off them, knock some off my arms and legs.

The younger boys tear out of the house to announce our good luck to the world. We can hear them through the open kitchen window screaming through the whole neighborhood:

Lard for sale. Grease for sale. Oil for sale.

Get those boys back in here, Vati says. Right now.

We don't want to let our secret out, he says, when I drag the little boys back into the kitchen. Let's not let anyone else in on this, all right? It's our monopoly. We'll clean up. Now let's try it out. Somebody make some pancakes, c'mon, c'mon.

The latest batch of wheat stolen from the monastery has been turned into flour just the day before. Heda mixes some with water. It clumps in a big wash bowl. Before I can stop them, snails float in the batter. I pick them out one by one. Start a fire, get out our biggest cast-iron frying pan. Any moment oil will come trickling out of the meat grinder.

Any moment now.

Then I'll heat that precious oil, spoon in the batter, fry up the best pancakes ever. So hurry up, we yell, our hunger pains always worse when food is close at hand. We're pacing from excitement, hopping, fidgeting.

Who will get the first taste?

Oh how delicious it will be. Fat sizzling in the pan, fried pancakes.

More snails, more snails. More damn snails, the boys chant. Even more snails are stuffed into the meat grinder that's harder to turn now. Stupid mess. The houses of the snails have gotten caught up in the inner workings of the grinder, are stopping it up. But somehow the older boys manage to turn the handle.

Somebody finds a new pan to collect the oil in. The first one has nothing but green-yellow juice in it that stinks. Guess that's just the contents of the snails' intestines. They're so big and fat. So it takes a while to get out their bad parts, purify their contents.

Once that's out of the way, the oil will start flowing.

Crank that thing, crank that thing, harder—harder.

Crank crank; crunch-crunch. The sound from all those snail houses being ground up.

But just think of the possibilities! Once we learn to separate the bad parts of the snails from their rich oils and have gorged ourselves on our scrumptious pancakes and have cooked up enough for the coming days, we can really go into the grease-producing business. We'll collect even more snails and slugs, all of them. Rid Bavaria of them, except for the fattest, best ones we'll keep for breeding purposes, all right? Then we'll grind them up day and night, collect all that oil. Learn to separate the slime from the real stuff. Maybe it'll float; we'll skim it off the top, or use a filter, sieve—whatever it takes. Then we'll become the biggest, baddest black marketeers ourselves!

Get back all our furniture. Yes, our heirlooms, paintings, jewelry, our heritage. Our name. Buy back all the beautiful things Mutti lugged from Magdeburg, the remnants of our fine home. Our past. We'll be *real* Vierlings again. Not starving pretenders.

Back to our noble past, dammit.

Ja, ja, ja! we think, filled with anticipation.

But the more squiggly snails Vati stuffs into the big meat grinder, the more awful juice dribbles out. It varies in color, sure, but stays thin and keeps smelling bad, worse. That's all.

And when we put some of it in the pan and heat it, then pour the pancake batter on it, it all gets ruined. The snail juice is just no good. There's not one drop of oil. The pancakes stick to the cast iron. Smoke, burn up—

Truth is, there's not one smidgen of anything resembling oil in the hundreds and hundreds of snails, fat or skinny, old or young, all those squiggly clumps. All those mountains of frenzied snails have nothing but stinking slime juice in them. Shit, snail diarrhea. So forget the pancakes, forget getting some breakfast, forget becoming famous black marketeers, forget being rich.

Forget everything.

But we still don't want to let go of our dream, spend all day collecting more snails, all different kinds. Force them into the groaning grinder. Now it takes three boys to turn the handle, then five. The crunching gets louder and louder. Ground snail houses come out along with the stinking juice. Ground snails come out too finally. They look like rotten hamburger meat.

Sickening.

Not even the bravest among us can choke that stuff down, cooked or raw.

Of course, we've ruined the grinder. And Julie who has been upstairs all this time working on her rag suit almost faints when she realizes it. Vati has long since left the kitchen, slamming the door behind him. It's my job to clean up the remains of the snail slaughter. I scrape the walls with a spatula while the little boys cry from hunger and disappointment.

When neighbors appear to buy some "oil," Julie meets them at the door. Her hair is combed neatly. She wears a ruched apron made from a flour sack that's been washed, laid out wet on the grass and been bleached by the sun. Sorry for the misunder-

standing. Oh you know our kids, they were just acting out a play. Please forgive them. So creative, well
yes, sure, they all are. Here have some of this. No,
just take it, take it.

She stills all complaints by giving away the last of
our flour. Now we have nothing.

But when she sees me, her brightly dancing eyes
stop and focus, and she bursts out screaming: What
do you think this is? A pigsty? Mop that floor, wipe
those counters down, scour those walls, boil water
and scrub all those dishes. Oh, my meat grinder. Real
Solingen steel, the last of all my fine kitchen utensils.
How could you? How could you?

She never hits me, doesn't have to.

Her words are whips.

Vati doesn't say anything that evening. How can
he? To be poor is bad. To have been well off and then
poor is worse. To have been well off, then poor, then
for a few glorious moments you thought you were
well off again—that can destroy you.

He looks it now. Since snails look slimy, he as-
sumed they'd have oil or fat tucked somewhere in
their bodies, at least a trace of it. But he was wrong.
He made a mistake.

What a grandmaster of mistakes he is.

How many others has he made? Will he make?

I know this is an omen. A bad one. Can't fall asleep
again that night. The little brothers moan from hunger;
the rest of my siblings are quiet but their legs move,
kick. Must be dreaming about running away.

I sure would if I were them, I think.

But mainly I think about life. Who made it this

way—so hard? I don't know what it was like to be well off; those days were before my time.

All I have ever known is having to scrounge around for food. But that's not so bad if you have the one thing you desperately need.

And that's like grease, really. Without some type of grease, you can hardly cook anything. So in life. You need something to make it if you have nothing. Especially if you have nothing. You need more than the figure of a father, mother, brothers, sisters, a roof over your head. Some rags to cover yourself with, some mattress to flop on at night.

You need some human grease, oil, lard, shortening. Whatever you might call it. You need something that makes the rest go easier. A pat on the head, once a year maybe. Or a little smile, just a half-smile. Maybe just a few good words. A drop of love.

Say, something like: Good job with cleaning up that awful kitchen!

Just someone to acknowledge what you did.

A gesture, hint. A tiny indication that you are.

That you exist.

If only Mutti hadn't died.

CHAPTER 10

Mystery Roast

ife is a never-ending foggy November—gray, slow. An eternal blur. Hunger dulls our senses. We kids withdraw, lose interest even in devilish pranks. It's another one of those many miserable days in the numbing weeks, months and years of hunger. We tossed and turned all night. Some of us cried out in the dark because of our hunger pains as always. More cries these days: There are now 10 of us: Heda, Hansi, Heini, Ger, Rudi, me, Paul, Joachim, Wolfi, Werner. Another baby will come shortly.

Won't Vati and Julie ever quit making kids, dammit?

How can we ever do better, if those babies keep coming? Whatever food we can scrounge up, it's never enough. So at night our bodies rebel the most. We're not only hungry, we have horrible nightmares. I often wake up in an icy sweat. I'm on the battle front, have to fight enemy soldiers, have no weapons. Bare hands only. I'm not a person, just some *thing*. When there are too many enemies, I run and run and still they catch me, those cruel soldiers, monsters, out to torture me. Hurt me, worse than the hunger pains.

But how can any pain be worse?

There are other pains, equal pains, sure, not that I've experienced them all, but I have a good imagination.

One time before the American and French occupation flooded our landscape, when the Russian army marched into Germany's Eastern regions, when they swallowed up the poor ruined city of Magdeburg and threatened to keep advancing, my father got out some rusty scissors and yelled, Heda, Ger, Eri, *komm her*.

Heda is 10 at the time, Ger, seven and I'm six.

Listen up, he says. The Russians aren't far away. If they come any closer, I'll cut off all your hair.

Why? I ask. Even then, I always *ask*.

So you look like boys. You'll have to wear your brothers' pants and shirts.

No, Vati, no, Ger cries. She has pretty hair. Blonde ringlets form a halo around her angel face, her soft cheeks.

I have no other choice, Vati says. The Russians treat little boys better than little girls.

Heda: Don't they kill the boys?

Sometimes, sure, but that's all they do to boys, not more. Little girls on the other hand....His voice trails off.

Heda seems to understand what he's talking about and folding her arms, steps up to him. Her chin juts out. She has pretty brown hair, bright intelligent eyes, an arresting face and knows a lot more than the rest of us, which she should at her age. Most of all she has guts and just calmly waits for those scissors to start clicking.

Since I have nothing but colorless clumps of matted fuzz for hair that's caked together from dirt and all those running sores my scratching produces, I don't mind getting my hair cut at all. Nor do I mind wearing my brother's pants. It'll be just another warm layer over my own clothes. So I eagerly step up to Vati. Me first.

But Ger is getting more and more upset. Why? she screams. She treasures her curls. Wants to be in the movies some day. Hollywood.

Because I'm trying to spare you, Vati says.

But the Russians stop advancing toward our region that day. The British stay to the north, and now both the American and French soldiers, who occupied our town for some time, have come and gone.

So our small town nestled into the most beautiful Bavarian landscape is left to its own devices again. That means the farmers still have something to eat. Their fertile plots of land bounce back. And God listens to the prayers of the nuns and priests. Their bumper crops never fail. It's like that fish story in the Bible—of course, their food never runs out.

But displaced city folks like us are starving to death. Educated becomes emaciated, for what good is the finest education now? My father's ground-breaking doctoral dissertation on semi-conductors, which caused a stir in 1933? The fact that his re-corded family history dates back eons? That his father doctored up all kinds of royalty? That he him-self is a walking encyclopedia? Can translate Latin into ancient Greek and vice versa?

And what good are all his damn inventions?

These days Vati's face is all sharp bones. The light eyes burn fiercely. He chews hard on his toothbrush the few times he strides up from his cellar lair. Julie's face is a collection of dark hollows into which she seems to have fallen. Her eyes are pitch-black ringed. She shakes a lot, and not only when there's thunder and lightning, which she always believes is another air raid or bombing attack, no matter how often we kids tell her: It's just a big storm. Please, stop it, please. See, no more bombs are falling from the sky?

But Julie's beyond reason at times like those. She shakes and trembles, clutches the torn tablecloth or her faded apron hard. It's a dying person's last grasp on a bed sheet. Don't even go near Julie then. She grabs you so tight, plucks at you as if you're a stub-born chicken whose feathers refuse to come out. Almost tears you apart.

But only her big hands are alive. Her light-blue eyes are dull, lead-colored, dead.

It's as if her strong fingers make a last desperate attempt to hold onto life

So this isn't a good time, a good month, a good year, a good decade. None of them are, the years after the war that take *so* long to pass.

The late 1940s, the early 1950s seem to stretch into a century.

All of us kids are suffering more than usual. We wander around sick and weak: Our skin is gray; the little brothers suck their knuckles. They're bleeding raw. Horseflies buzz around, waiting for us to sink down somewhere, not get up again. Then they'll settle on us, feed off our sores, lay their eggs on us.

The only living things that still look healthy are the rats in town.

Whether they're feasting on corpses that still haven't been claimed is often discussed, but no matter. Shrugs go round. Who cares where the rats get their food?

It's poor people like us who need meat and potatoes desperately.

In despair Vati sets out traps for the big rats, but has nothing for bait. So the fat rats aren't tempted to go near the traps. On the contrary, they just get more and more brazen. They dance in front of the beloved ancient cat the neighbors own, and that poor thing can't catch any of them. We can't either.

Yet we kids can't just sit and vegetate, go on and starve in peace. No, every morning we have to get up and go to school. Learn something, memorize long passages, be brilliant like our Vati. The family tradition must go on. In the midst of the worst famine, the Catholic nuns patch up the bombed-out roof section of a building next to their church, sweep away the rubble and open school again.

From the moment I step into the small hut, I love it. I'm not a cripple in the classroom, no rickets matter here. Who cares if you're the family coward?

For once I'm away from all that pain that lives at my house. I don't have to see my father turn bonier each day and Julie sink into herself like a melting snowman. And listen to their fighting, which escalates year by year. No matter how weary they get, they're never too weary to fight. Fight fiercely.

The curses between them fall like lightning.

But school—what a haven. Once or twice we even get something to eat there. One incredible day an American lady comes to visit. Not Eleanor Roosevelt after whom I'm named, but another American lady. In funny German she tells us: Run home and get a paper bag, now.

I sprint home as fast as I can, shouting: I need a paper bag bad. We're going to get some food at school. An Ami lady has come.

Julie looks at me, shrugs. I run to the cellar. Vati, Vati. I need a paper bag. Please, hurry.

We don't have any paper bags. Not one.

Since we have no money we can never buy anything from any stores even if one were open. What paper bags we once had have long since been used for toilet paper.

But I don't give up. Please, Vati, please. A paper bag.

He realizes how desperate I am, searches through the house, finds a sheet of old newspaper in the attic. Out comes the slide rule, the sharpened pencil, some glue almost dried in a tube. He figures, measures. Measures, figures. Scribbles numbers on scraps of paper, multiplies numbers, gets root squares, works furiously.

Then he cuts precisely, folds, glues. Here.

I run back to school, relieved when I see the Ami

lady is still there. Dozens of kids line up and as the lady walks down the line dispensing what she brought us, every child in town holds out a bag. Some are ancient, some wrinkled, some huge, some small, some torn, some taped together. But every child has an ordinary brown or beige paper bag.

Except for one child. Me.

I hold up a stunning masterpiece—a little home-made bag that's precisely constructed of newspaper. Creased just so, it has a headline and date from the 1920s running around the edge.

The class bursts into screams of laughter at the sight. I feel on fire from the top of my head to my toes, want to sink into the floor. Having no bag would have been better than this. No wonder I often get strange looks from my classmates. They think Vati is weird; we are all weird. Those crazy Vierlings.

Don't we carry our old violin in a soap-box car?

❦ ❦ ❦

All this *Scheisse!* my brothers say when we have to take private music lessons. Why do we have to keep pretending the family is still what it was before the war? Why do all of have to be good skiers, skaters, swimmers, platform divers, sailors, canoers, plus play the piano, flute, guitar, zither, and now the violin?

We don't have the sports equipment, the musical instruments or the money to buy them. Why can't we just lounge around and do nothing? We are nothing. So let us be, dammit.

All this forced activity requires more energy than we have. What little food we get is barely enough to keep us going. It's never enough for all those extra pursuits we're forced into.

Vati is relentless though. He has no job, is home all the time, makes no money, gets no food on the table. But he has no trouble at all finding lonely old women and men who thrive on torturing us with their private lessons. We kids resent these added duties and do our best to get out of them. The boys are masterful at it.

When their piano teacher makes them take off their shoes when they enter her house for their lessons, they promptly escape through the window when she's not looking, run home on socks, resulting in more giant holes for me to mend.

Next time, they spend the night outdoors, scaring everyone because we think they have really run away this time. So no more lessons for them for the next few weeks. Lucky rascals.

But I'm dumb and can never think of a good way to get out of stuff.

I have a sense of duty lodged in my throat, a stupid inner voice that won't shut up.

Where that ugly old violin I get stuck with is from, I don't know, but I have to take lessons. OK, just dump it into a rucksack, I tell Vati, defeatedly. I dread the thought of having to stand in front of a creepy old teacher and screech out some melody while my stomach's bound to rumble nonstop.

But no, no. Vati is in his element. No violin in a rucksack. What do you think we are? Uncultured? Uncivilized?

He scours the town for some boards and other pieces of lumber. Out come the pencil and slide rule. Again there's all kinds of serious measuring and figuring. Inventing in progress. First it looks like he's making me a little wagon. Vati saws and sands, screws and glues, polishes and pats. In no time cracked shoe-leather hinges, which he fashions just so and paints lovingly, connect the clumsy lid of the soapbox car with the odd-looking bottom. A piece of blue-and-red checked flannel night gown lines the inside, under which he pokes shredded underpants for cushioning. A ragged piece of an old snake-skin belt is hammered to the side for a handle.

Then he sets his "violin case" on the floor. It looks like a little boy put it together. Maybe it should be entered in a race.

Here you go, Vati says, eyes alive. Another brilliant invention completed.

But I shiver, hot from shame. *Ach Gott.* Does he really expect me to carry the violin in this soapbox car?

My face stays flushed. Just looking at this awkward contraption is humiliating. And it's so sharp-cornered and much too big to cover with a coat, so I have to carry it out in the open. In public. Every week I have to carry this object of pain down the street to the violin teacher's house. It's such a mark of disgrace, announcing to the whole world how far we've sunk.

We're such failures we can't even accept our failure. Plus we're crazy. Instead of quitting at the top, or fizzling out at the bottom and fading away quietly, we're a pitiful sick bunch long past its prime, trying to make a pathetic comeback. And what the hell for?

Families rise and families fade or fall all the time. We Vierlings got our asses whipped by the war.

So why can't we stay down and out? It's all over with us.

I sigh. But no, Vati won't see it my way. And there's no back way for me to get to the violin teacher's house, no other route.

So I sneak down the street, trying to hide the ugly box. It's hard to carry. The hard leather handle cuts into my hand. The sharp edges of the wooden box bump into my leg, and there are always other kids out. They're just like me—skinny, hollow-eyed, looking for food.

But that's where the similarities end.

Those other kids get to hang in the gutter, wear their rags openly, curse to their heart's content, just are good and trashy. I have to hustle to my violin lesson, then run home again, cook and clean, dust, do laundry. I have to wear my old rags washed and mended, my hair done up in tight braids. Have to take a bath every week or every other week, then put on fresh underwear that's homemade and scratches between my skinny legs, rubs me raw. Sack cloth doesn't get soft even if you boil it a hundred times.

Yet no matter how I suffer, those other kids have no mercy on me. Hey, what you got there? A damn race car? They taunt me. Can I drive it? Are you carrying some liquor? Let's have a look. Shoot, are you packing some pistols?

They try to take the big box away from me. I have to struggle to hold on. They tug and throw rocks at me. Shit. Think you're better than us—ha ha ha.

No. I know I'm worse than they are. They are comfortable in their world. I'm not because mine is insane.

So wish I could be one of them, just once, sit on the curb, pee in the gutter, pick off my lice at leisure. Dig in my nose, peel off scabs. Fart, fight, and bite.

But no. I have to take these dumb lessons in shame every week. No matter how weak I am, I have to hustle to the teacher's house on time. Have no money to pay for the sheet music, nor can I pay for broken strings. So I have to make up excuses, beg to let me pay next time, scrape my feet, mumble something, butter the teacher up with fake compliments. Act meek, grateful for any extensions of the fees. Could I maybe do your dishes? Be your maid?

Clean your house to pay in exchange?

I take home their sheet music and copy it by hand, stay up late and do their mending too, hating every stitch I have to make.

Enough, enough already. Let me out of those lessons.

I hate everything about them. But no way out. I have to tune the violin, wax the frazzled bow, coax some awful noises out of my instrument of embarrassment, all the while trying to figure out a different route home, so I won't run into those kids again. They're just regular dirty, filthy post-war kids enjoying their lice and life.

I'm the odd one, the weirdo.

Can't even climb over back fences on my way home because I'm wearing the only outfit I have. I have just one. It's what I wear to school and church, where now the precious relics are out in full force again. Now that the worst of the occupation is over, the churches have emptied their crypts again and all the saints under glass are back in their places. Giant gold-leaf crosses, polished to blinding pomp, adorn the altars. Jewel-encrusted chalices are lifted heavenward, gilded angels rise in cupolas, organ pipes burst into proud song again. Bells toll. Incense wafts while the parishioners pray. Germany is on the move again, out of the ashes....Up. Up.

I go to church since I'm forced to, but I don't pray. I'm too *verdammt* busy thinking: How much could all those shimmering doodads bring on the black market? How many kids could get some food for once?

Wouldn't those precious purple priests' robes make nice dresses? Something to wear for that silly dance class I'm now forced to attend as well. It's my latest torture. All "higher" daughters have to know society stuff, see, like how to do ballroom dances, as if we'd ever get invited to a big party. It's idiotic to even think about that happening.

And even if it would, what would I wear?

So I hide behind the other girls in dance class. Don't want anyone to see the ragged outfit I have on. The worst time is when the girls and the boys have class together. The girls stand along one wall, shy and giggly. The boys line up against the opposite wall, red-faced and clumsy. When the sign is given, the boys bite their lips, advance toward the girls, eyes on the floor. They mumble something, grab a girl's hand. Step woodenly to the center of the room, then the dancing starts. Marionettes carved by a bungling puppet-maker. Step-step-step with stiff legs, wooden expressions. But after a while the dancing gets better. Some of the couples relax; a twirling begins here and there like a pot of soup starting to boil. Other kids start circling. The waltz music is winding them up. A polka makes them pounce.

A tango tames them.

The boys are still red-faced but now from the exertion. The girls are pliable. Smiles appear. But it's never ever fun for me. I always slink behind the line of girls, hoping no boy will discover me, ask me to dance. When one does anyway, even though I shake my head, ignore his outstretched hand, and mumble that I'm sick, I step on the dance floor as if it's ice. Take tiny awkward steps. It's not that I can't do the dance. But the skirt I'm wearing is the best one I have. My sister Ger and I share it. Luckily she has her lessons another day.

The skirt is dark-blue shimmering taffeta, the right length. But the problem is with the pleats. They look fine as long as I stand still or mince along. But when I take bigger steps or when I turn, the skirt puffs up, the hem flares out, and all the pleats open up, like a big flower. But the pleats are torn. They're long ugly slits and reveal my ragged underwear. Those tears are too numerous to mend. Each new needle stitch causes another rip. So all I can do is dance as stiffly as possible. I'm an arthritic circus bear, clomp, clomp, clomp. I step on the boy's shoes, hoping he'll learn his damn lesson and never ask me again for a dance—good.

Maybe next time I can hide in the bathroom.

In May we have a big dance to celebrate the conclusion of the class. Of course, I'm not going. Never go to anything. For years in school when the teacher mentions a field trip, a visit to the museum, a meeting after class, going on a picnic, seeing a movie, a play, attending a concert, I always have the same answer: I can't go. Either my parents are sick and need me at home, or they don't believe in my taking part in such frills—those are my stock answers.

The real reason is always: We don't have the money. Even if the event is free, it takes money for a bus ride. Or the streetcar. Or we're asked to pack a snack. I can go hungry for a long time, for days, but not when all my classmates unpack ham sandwiches, boiled eggs, soft drinks, chocolate cookies. All of them have only one or two siblings and parents who at least tolerate each other, at least coexist. They have the bare necessities. I never do.

That May dance. I can't go, I say immediately, but this time my girlfriends gang up on me. You must come, you must. Must. Please, please, please. I have a dress you can have. I have an extra pair of shoes.... And so on.

Stupid me, vain me. Silly me. I let them persuade me to go this once, wash myself in the cold water at home. We have hot water sometimes but never when I need it. I also wash my hair, rinse it in vinegar, roll it on sections of rubber hose, pin it with wire twists, squeeze into the borrowed dress. It doesn't close in the back. What can you expect?

I am tall and the years of hard labor have put muscles on me. But if I hold my breath, suck my stomach in with all my might, I can get the dress zipped up. One careless breath and the zipper breaks, just a little so far. But Ger sews the zipper together and me into the dress.

Just take tiny breaths, all right? she says. Why're you so pale? What's the matter?

I feel all squished together and can't talk. Talking means I might relax, start to breathe normally. That would make the thread break and the zipper would come apart all the way.

Ger pulls out an empty lipstick tube dug out of a garbage heap, coaxes out the remnants of color with a twig, rubs them on my cheeks. Here you go, you're beautiful.

Thank you, Ger. I feel my eyes water.

But I'm not beautiful. I'm a mummy trussed into a too-tight, floor-length, peach dress with ruffles all over. My face is white with bright-red clown's cheeks contrasting to the dark circles under my eyes. I have to walk with my toes curled so I won't lose those borrowed shoes I have on. They're two sizes too big.

But off we go, all of us girls, to the dance where a boy leads me out on the floor and twirls me around. Maybe someone put him up to it: Ask the ugliest girl for the first dance.

But I surprise him. Ha! I can do all those steps easily, can keep up with the music, do the foxtrot with flair. In a mirrored wall far in the distance, I can see myself floating with this boy in his new suit and tie. I'm tall with a face that's mostly bones and planes. But the overhead light softens their harshness. My dark hair fluffs around my face and shines for the first time ever. And the peach dress paints color on my skin. The dark circles under my eyes fade.

For one split second I'm pretty.

Which makes me forget the dress's limitations. I

exhale fully, inhale just as fully——Rrrtsch! I feel a cold draft on my chest and stomach. My face is on fire. The dress has split down in front all the way.

I tear from the dance hall. Home, run home, hide under my bed. Won't cry until I get there. No trouble. I take off those big shoes and start walking, I can walk many kilometers. Munich is a vast city with wide sidewalks. The war rubble has been cleared away, and new stone blocks sprout from the ruins. Every day another new gray building shoots up, its windows cold flat eyes. In a few short years, all signs of the war will be covered up. The wounds of war will be patched up seamlessly, but just the outer ones.

After covering my front with discarded newspaper, I put new block after new block behind me.

I'm glad Mutti didn't have to see this!

Takes a long time for the fire in my face to go down.

🐛 🐛 🐛

Often complete strangers wander up to our house, which looks normal from the outside and not like the insane asylum it's turning into. They stop at our gate. Julie invites them in. They gape at the many beds, some swinging from the ceiling in the hall like hammocks. Another one of Vati's inventions.

The people are always in awe and say to Julie: Oh, how wonderful, you're a saint, so many kids, how do you do it? They gush on, clap their hands. Can we take a picture of them?

When Vati is home, he whistles and trained like dogs, we kids fall into formation. All 10, then 11 of us.

We know the routine by now: Look your best if it kills you. Wear your one presentable outfit. Make sure the holes are pinned together out of view.

We turn our socks so the holes aren't visible. March so our missing shoe soles aren't noticeable. Have our hair slicked back with spit. Braids pinned back with old wire. All obvious lice picked off, quick, quick. Scabs hidden. Heda winds a scarf around her neck so the moth-eaten top of her sweater's out of sight.

Can't you smile, please, the visitors ask, getting their cameras ready. This is something. Germany's risen from the ashes. Just look at all those handsome kids.

The older kids do smile and some of the younger ones. It's painful smiles mostly. But not me. Never me.

I don't smile. Does a wild animal that's paraded around in a circus, then locked up, tortured and starved over and over, smile?

And what about all those poor people killed in Dachau?

Can they smile?

I want to scratch the visitors' eyes out. Charge at Vati and Julie. Scream: Why are we playing this game? Why's everybody acting as if the war was a natural disaster, a cyclone that touched down out of the sky, like those bombs wiping out Magdeburg?

Five years ago not far from here some people gassed some other people. Stuffed them into ovens. Burned them to a crisp. Insanity—and I am supposed to smile?

And anyway, Julie "doesn't do it." Nobody really

does. It's mainly Ger and me who "do it," whatever gets done around here. Sure, Julie supervises, organizes, criticizes.

Is she good at that.

And Vati. Oh Vati. He only remembers how it was when he grew up. When there were upstairs maids and downstairs maids, and chauffeurs, butlers. Music tutors came to the house and gave piano lessons. When the laundresses came on Monday, the bakery delivered every day, the cook made the best *apfelstrudel* in the area, the large household was run by a competent staff. Nannies and baby nurses took care of the kids. And Oma wore white gloves, ran them across the fine armoires to see if any dust was overlooked on the way out to her teas or to another lovely march in support of the women's right to vote. Germany in the 1920s. What is was to be upper-class and spoiled back then. In the evening, coifed and swathed in silks and satins, and doused in the finest fragrances, my much admired grandmother presided over galas.

Tables wrapped in snowy linen groaned under golden trays of caviar, roast duckling, stuffed baked trout, shrimp remoulade, goose liver pate, Westphalian ham, prosciutto, brie, camembert, white asparagus, strawberries dipped in chocolate....

Her filthy, scabby grandchildren dream of a crust of bread.

❦ ❦ ❦

Not all days are bad. Every year or two, there's a good one. They're forever etched in my mind. For example, on the day of food handouts back at school in Diessen, when I'm the only one without a regular paper bag, the Ami lady compensates me for my embarrassment. Gives me an extra scoop when she doles out her wonderful little presents, puckered little purple gems. They taste like the essence of the world's sweetness is collected in them. Raisins. I've never had one before. They're so good I cry when the last one slips down my throat. Wish I could vomit it up so I can eat it again. I hurt never again getting a raisin until a decade later.

A real raisin—what bliss.

Another time we get a free sip of milk at school. Another American lady comes, sends us home for a cup. Oh, oh, we have cups. Lots of ordinary chipped, cracked cups. Vati doesn't have to make me one out of clay! Paint it like a Rembrandt.

Yes, it's incredible when we get some food at school. The American ladies are creatures from another planet. Exquisite, big china figurines sprung to life. And I'm starstruck. Remember my mother's admiration of Eleanor Roosevelt. Maybe some day I'll read a book about America, that place of mystery. We have no books in our school, just long makeshift benches in a dark hut, on which I crowd along with all the other village kids.

Whatever Sister explains I try to do exactly. We learn to add and subtract on shards of slate. Practice writing our first letters on cardboard pieces, dirty paper scraps. Every time I bite my lip and try to do my very best, even hold still when Sister washes my neck and ears after class, which happens often. She doesn't like it when we're too dirty.

One time she scrubs my bottom. Never getting food regularly, my stomach has forgotten what to do.

My intestines become contrary. Once I find a slice of bread before school. Cram it all down in one swoop. Then the worst that can happen to a kid in school does. Diarrhea leaks from me in front of the whole class. They laugh, box each other, and laugh more. Where's your damn hot rod car when you need it, a boy yells. You could *scheissen* in that.

I want to die.

But Sister just keeps me after school, brings a white enamel bowl with lukewarm water to the bench to which I'm caked and starts cleaning me up.

She scrubs and prays over me. Many fervent prayers over my filthy behind. My dark soul too.

During class when some kids whisper or write messy or won't keep their arms folded just so, their backs ramrod straight, Sister is vicious. Out comes her hissing ruler and bites into the open palms of the kids who don't behave. They have to hold out their hands and try not to wince when she whacks them. Whack-thwack! But that's never me. I'm quiet as a mouse.

More quiet. Because on the long way home from school, I now see armies of mice and rats playing openly in the fields. Brazenly they chitter and nobody's able to stop them.

One day after school again, I drag my feet, dawdle along the winding dirt path. I want to delay coming home to our house of horror. There's always a crisis, another calamity, total chaos. Screams, shouts.

But today it's like a holiday. Everybody's bouncing around the kitchen where a fire crackles in the big cast-iron monster of a range that's been dark and cold for months now.

Vati's finally had some luck with the traps. He's set rusty steel-jaw traps everywhere.

A rabbit, a rabbit. Vati caught a big fat rabbit, tralalala. The brothers sing and scream, jump up and down. Everybody's scrambling for a seat around the table, and the smell of cooking, the aroma of the roast, is incredible. We're still jostling for seating space when Julie takes the roasting pan out of the oven.

Voices clamor to be heard: Can I lick out the pan? Can I? Can I? Can I have the lid? The spoon? Me. Me. Me.

No, I called it first. No, I'm the oldest. But I'm the youngest. I'm the hungriest. I'm the sickest—

I'm the strongest. Beat your damn ass if you don't get out of my way. Scat, scram....My older brothers' voices win out.

Finally I manage to peek between my siblings and see a roast the size of my father's fist holding forth in the pan. What a disappointment. Must've been a baby rabbit. But no matter, it's something to eat. Fortunately there's gravy in the pan too, a dark brown liquid that looks heavenly. Mouthwatering. But how can such a small roast feed us all?

Oh please, don't forget about me, I wail. Heda, as the oldest, has made sure she's not forgotten. But Ger, watching everyone else demand a bite, shakes her head. Uh-uh. I'm not hungry, she says, sniffing the air.

Can I have your piece? Can I? Can I? Can I?

It's a litany that echoes through the house as Ger leaves the kitchen, and Julie tries to get the rest of us kids to sit down so she can slice up the bounty.

I close my eyes in anticipation, deep breaths, get ready, open my eyes. Here it comes, my one little sliver of meat. Slow, I nibble it, savor it. I eat in one bite, dip my finger in the little dab of gravy I get and linger over each droplet. Then lick my plate, my fingers, my hands, manage to grab the lid of the roasting pan where condensation has deposited oh so many flavorful drops. A whole dozen of them, mine, all mine. I rejoice, lick the lid over and over. Hug it to my heart.

What a *wunderbar* life!

Next time I go up in the attic, I see a new piece of soft fur dangling from a nail, like a rag. It's from the neighbor's old cat.

Ger claims that's why she didn't want any of that roast.

She smelled cat.

🐞 🐞 🐞

But real food is appearing again here and there. Farmers have bountiful crops. We're on bad terms with most of them. So we don't get anything edible, unless we steal it. That's harder now because the more the farmers have, the more watchful they are. In school, the farmers' kids have round cheeks and some meat on their arms and legs. We have pointy chins, dark circles under our eyes, stick arms and legs even though we wear several pairs of kneesocks. So we don't get made fun of. Also we're cold. Being hungry makes you shiver a lot.

But one farmer has a heart for us hungry kids or an eye for beautiful Julie. He lets us come get some buttermilk once a week. Come in the back way.

That's Heini's bailiwick. The oldest of Julie's boys, he's shorter than Heda and Hansi but not much. While they are dark haired and brown eyed, he's blond and blue eyed, has a rakish curl on his forehead. He slicks it back with spit, and stomps around. Wish my mother had stayed in burned-out Cologne.

Why should he have to share what little food Julie can scrounge up with all those other kids, especially those Vierlings? Isn't it enough that all the furniture and household goods she brought into the marriage have long been sold on the black market? That Julie's diamond rings and fur coats went for a few slices of *wurst*? A thimbleful of sugar?

Well, he's the eldest of *her* boys. He'll see to it that her life will be easier. Rounding up a large metal milk can and a rickety hand wagon, or in the winter a sled, he takes over the hauling of the buttermilk. That's one thing that'll be done right.

Heini and one of his younger brothers set out. They pull the wagon, or sled, on which the large metal can bounces. They stroll through town and up the hill, on top of which the kind farmer lives. When the milk can is filled to the brim, he sits on top of it, has the little brother climb on his shoulders, then he heads back down the hill, in the middle of the busy street that slices the town in half.

Yeehaw—here we come. Heini has tied a rope to the handle of the wagon, yanks on it—giddyap!—like a cowboy.

The wagon zooms down the hill on wobbly wheels. Cars screech to a stop, people jump out of the way. The buttermilk brigade shoots past. Heini never loses control, brings the wagon to a smooth stop at the bottom of the hill down by the lake. From there he pulls it along the lake's edge, then back up *Krankenhausweg* outside of town to our ruin. As his prize, he slurps half the buttermilk right out of the can.

He has near misses, but never spills a drop of the buttermilk. He walks with a swagger and his curl's always in place when he comes home. Another successful haul.

True, sometimes one of the younger brothers flies off his shoulders, especially if they have to skirt an oncoming car, some out-of-towner who's not aware that Wednesdays at 4 PM it's best to pull over. Wait for Heini's buttermilk wagon or sled to whoosh by.

The little boys get a tooth or two knocked out. No problem. Our teeth are loose anyway. Or they may end up with a black eye. Or a broken arm or leg. But none of those things matter. There are always more little brothers begging for the thrilling ride through town, high up on Heini's shoulders, the wind whizzing past their ears.

Just like the French soldiers' bullets used to.

Besides the buttermilk, we get lucky in other ways. That Christmas we get a CARE package from the United States. It bulges with cans of horse meat meant for dogs. Some dear soul in America is worried about all the starving dogs in Germany.

But the only people who still have dogs are the nuns, and they have enough food for themselves plus their dogs.

Julie's face lights up at the package. Dress up, she says as she concocts elaborate dinners of noodles and precious bits of that horse meat. Those are the most delicious holiday meals I can remember. A whole plate of noodles with a sliver of stringy horse meat clinging to every tenth noodle. Just enough to give you hope you might find another meat morsel deep in the noodle pile.

Oh, how we feast.

Everything great in our lives comes from America.

So we make it another month and another. The bleak years drag on, but somehow we children manage to get enough food to grow. In summer the boys dive for mussels in the lake, which they pry open, bite off whatever they find inside the shells, eat it raw. Heda wants us girls to get part of the action too. Ger can swim, so no problem. Dive down to the lake bottom, grab what you find. Bring it up.

But I'm slow. I didn't learn to swim at six or seven like all the others. Julie's kept me at home slaving, but that's not all. I don't have that dare devil spirit my siblings have. When I watch them don their homemade skis, pieces of boards that are pointed, and shoot down an icy cliff in winter, I have no desire to follow suit like Heda, like Ger.

On unmatched skis strapped to some old shoes of Vati's, which they slip on, they sail down any mountain, no matter how high. They skate figure-eights for hours on the lake, can outrun any other youngster in town.

When a traveling circus comes to Diessen, Heda beats the circus kids at every event, from walking a tightrope, to doing perfect handstands, to insane bicycle stunts. No matter what the circus kids think up, Heda's way ahead of them.

Ger watches the impromptu contest, raises her hands up, bends like a switch backwards until she touches the floor. Then she forces her head back even more until she can grab her ankles and hold on to them. She's twisted herself backwards into a standing circle.

And smiles brilliantly.

Disgusted, the circus kids give up trying to compete with us.

And when Ger climbs onto the ancient diving platform that rises by the lake as high as a church steeple, spreads her arms and takes flight, I hold my breath. She soars straight into nothing for a couple of seconds. Bends sharply at the waist, then heads down. Dips into the clear lake water without a splash. Emerges again shortly all excited.

A graceful beauty, an athletic swan, a bathing ballerina.

I climb up on that platform too, but only once. Look around. The deep blue lake below me, the green rolling hills dotted with churches behind the lake.

For a moment I'm a child, scared about the height but excited too. Then in the distance behind the hills, I see white wisps pasted on the limitless sky. Are they soft little clouds or remnants of the Dachau smokestacks?

I shake my head. Oh God! Climb down from the tower. Why jump off that high place if there's a perfectly good ladder?

More importantly, why waste energy on all these

diversions when important things have to be pondered, such as life and death?

And justice.

Justice and Jews.

Why?

Why was Dachau allowed to happen?

CHAPTER 11

German Swine

In addition to the forced marches, Vati believes in vacations. But what they are are nightmares. Two or three or four weeks of forced marches up and down some very steep hills and no food at all. And not once sleeping in a bed or anything resembling one the whole time.

Our vacations start as soon as the post-war economy gets on its feet again in the early 1950s. When I'm 11 or 12, Vati finally gets a job, his first one after WW II. He's had work before, of course. After the war, all German men who are able to walk are ordered to clear the streets of rubble. The pay is minimal, but it gets folks working again.

One day there's more than rubble to clear away. Hansi and the other boys race home screaming: We're rich. Their hands clutch piles of money— German marks in huge denominations. It's all over everywhere, they shout. Money rained from heaven.

We girls run into town and rake the bills together like leaves. Stuff all the cash we can into our shirts, underpants. Stagger home drunk with elation. We're millionaires.

The money's worthless and only good for starting a fire. New money's coming out, and each family gets a small amount, something worth five or ten dollars. And soon stores open again with real goods, and people start shopping again.

I haven't been inside a store with supplies on shelves in years and tiptoe into a small grocery. It's a miracle to see those packed shelves. What a sight. There are new boxes of crackers. Shiny cans of fruit and soup. Gleaming jars of jam. Tightly packed sacks of flour and sugar. I want to hug them all. Press them to my heart.

Oh, there are even bottles of golden oil. And tubs of snowy white lard. Incredible how many kinds of fat exist in this wonderful new world: There's pork fat and chicken fat; olive oil and sunflower oil. And more kinds of animal and vegetable grease.

It's like Christmas. I reach for a bottle of shimmering oil. My hands shake. I check the price. It's the same amount as what we got when the money changed. So buying one bottle of oil would wipe us out financially. I put the bottle back on the shelf; discover something better. A refrigerated display case. *Ach du lieber Gott!* Look! It's crammed full of bricks of margarine and butter.

From then on, I race to the grocery store after school every day to window-shop. I stand in front of the cold case and gape at the offerings. With my eyes

I caress the different kinds of margarine, count the various brands. Feast on the buttercup yellow of the butter. Drink in the pale waxy look of the margarine.

Someday when I have money, I will buy a pound of each and gorge myself.

Now of course, we can never buy anything that luxurious. Real groceries from a real store? Out of the question. If we're lucky, a butcher tosses a slab of fat-back out the back door at us. We snatch it, race home with it. Fry it until it's crunchy. The drippings are so good on bread, if we have some.

But we never have any extra money to waste on groceries, even now. There are just too many of us. Eleven kids, no matter how often you count. But Vati progresses from the rubble cleaning to a job in a factory and brings in a little more money. But it's never enough. In all the years I knew my father, he never had enough money for the basic necessities of his family. He never earned enough to feed his brood.

Still, Vati takes two of the brand-new bills from his first factory paycheck and tucks them deep into his wallet, which one of us found for him in the trash. For the next catastrophe, he says. WW III. We'll always, always have this, understand? So next time we won't starve. We'll plan ahead and hoard some lard, all right? Stock up on oil.

We kids shrug. Who can worry about another war and what starvation that might bring? Hey. We're still starving now. In a good week, Vati earns enough for a family of three or four, but never enough for a family of 13 people, who all have all kinds of needs. One is wanting to eat at least one meal a day. Another is that we kids are growing and always need clothes. And that's not even mentioning shoes. Or medicine. Or glasses. Or going to a dentist. Or supplies for school.

Or personal stuff.

Real personal.

Like what we girls need once a month or more often. In my case, every three weeks. The few diapers we have are always in use. The little brothers pee oceans. Even after they should be trained, they still need diapers. So sadly, using diapers is out of the question.

And the boys' socks have been mended so much that they're stiff and scratch. They'd be all right otherwise. I'd have to use several at a time because my flow is always heavy. My periods plague me every time I turn around.

But the boys, eight of them now, don't have any socks to spare. We don't have extra towels either that we girls could cut up. Use, then wash, dry and use again. Same goes for sheets. There are barely enough for all the beds and cots crammed into our three small bedrooms and the hallways.

So what should I use for my periods? My girl-friends moan about their monthly cramps. Or how having dumb periods keeps them from whatever activities their mothers won't let them participate in during those days. Or how unfair this is: Girls have to have them, boys don't. La-de-da. Lucky girls.

For me it's always a huge crisis: What in heaven's name do I use this time?

The toilet paper we have at home—crumpled up scrap paper or cut-up old newspapers—doesn't absorb the flow. And it's so bulky when you fold it to make yourself a homemade Kotex. I have to walk funny, and it chafes the insides of my thighs. Still the flow soaks right through my underpants and skirt. In class, I can always tell by looking at my classmates that they're paying attention to the teacher or are daydreaming.

Wish I could indulge in either, but I don't have those choices. No. I always have to be on edge. Always have to worry: When it's time to get up and leave the classroom, how big will the red stain be on the back of my dress? What do I do when the flow runs down my leg? When I leave blood stains on the seat of my desk? When I'm called to the front of the room and dammit! I know the answers. But as I write the correct date on the board, what will I do when a pool of blood collects between my holey shoes?

This takes some serious planning, but I can manage. Somehow. What you do is be first in your seat and never budge. Never volunteer to come to the front of the room. Every year train the new teacher. Pretend you're too shy, sick, uncooperative. Act dumb, dumber, dumbest. Then you won't ever be called on to get up and read your report.

Next learn to control your bladder. Be ruthless. Then you'll never have to go to the bathroom during class when the other kids would have a chance to check out the back of your clothes, OK?

And stay after class every day. Mumble something. Wait until the teacher leaves, then sneak out. Hope and pray the hall is dark. By then you know you're flooding. You're dripping all over the floor. In the dark hall the blood spots look like oil slicks or ink-blots or spilled water.

The blood spots follow you, so hurry. Hurry.

Before anyone can come to investigate, rush to the nearest restroom. Beg God that the school's toilet paper supply is in abundance.

Sometimes it is. Great. It's always brown and the consistency of sandpaper. But a dozen layers wadded up can hold you until your next stop. That's going to be the back pews of St. Anna's Church, which you walk past on your way home. Some of the hymnals have blank pages, tear them out. Use them to reinforce the wad of paper. Then on to the next stop. The restroom of the *Drei Kronen Gasthaus* where maybe an old cleaning rag is hanging under the bathroom sink to dry. Ditch the soggy paper wad. Bunch up the cleaning rag. Somehow make it home where you can plot your next move.

But what if there's no toilet paper at school? None? You're trapped in the bathroom. The janitor's coming around. Slamming doors in the halls, locking up. And your underpants, the only pair you own, are soaked through. Your skirt has a dark stain the size of your palm in back. Then what?

And don't dare dawdle. Julie's waiting at home for you to get there, start your chores. Hop to it. In your mind you can hear her screaming already.

In that case you sacrifice something. Maybe your blouse. Wear your cardigan buttoned up all the way like a sweater. Which frees up your blouse. Which you then bunch up and stick in your underpants. Fasten it with safety pins.

Or take off your underpants, fold them so the clean parts can absorb more blood. Then use a piece of rope or a belt to strap the "pad" on you.

All right. Now you're on your way home.

Fortunately sometimes all you have to do is wait a little. Menstrual blood dries fast. Then you pull your skirt around, so the stain is in front of you. Hold your school books so the stain is covered. Head for the church, praying an old lady left a shawl behind.

Ha!

Even if she didn't, you can rest a while. The pews are upholstered in rich red velvet. Stains don't show. What a relief.

Finally at home, you vow to do better next time. Wear more clothes so you can sacrifice more. Steal your brothers' underpants. Hoard school toilet paper in your pocketbook. Swipe cleaning rags from all kinds of places—train stations, gas stations, back entrances of shops.

Wash them, dry them, stash them.

What a good feeling to have a stack of clean rags tucked under your mattress and it's still *two days* before your next period. And should you ever get your hands on a new skirt, pick one with a busy pattern on a red background, if you can. Hides the blood stains so much better than a solid-color one.

So dealing with my periods is tough but can be managed.

What can't be managed is our summer vacations.

Why does Vati think it's easier to feed 11 kids out in nature, when he can't do it at home? Why does he think we can just live off the land in Austria?

The land's been picked clean by the starving Austrians. There's nothing except beauty, and you sure can't eat that. Try stuffing a piece of azure sky in your mouth.

Still we pack a hand-sewn tent with canvas about to give up the ghost and a rusty knife. An aluminum frying pan, a dented pot, a few bent spoons and forks, a ragged blanket or two. And the clothes we have on our backs, sometimes extra canvas....

South we head, south. To the Austrian Alps where the air is fresh and the scenery is even prettier than in Bavaria and where being hungry is just as bad. Or worse. The outdoors always wakes up the beast in our bellies. The hunger monster. Vati doesn't think about that. His mind's on his brilliant inventions.

Off, off we go. *Komm, komm!* His voice is a strong net hauling us in. *Komm!* We hate Vati's vacations with a passion, but can't escape.

Early during WW II when Hitler confiscated all civilian cars, Vati drove his into an old garage, piled boxes and cardboard around it. The old Opel hasn't run in years and years, but now it's the new Germany, isn't it? The country's rising again out of the ruins. Up, up and up. Vati pushes the decrepit vehicle out of hiding, patches it up with wire, pieces of tin, curtain rods, electric tape. Bits of red and blue rope.

The end result is an embarrassing old heap that hates to be awakened from its slumber. We 11 kids squeeze in, which is painful. We have no money for gas, of course. So cursing, Vati has to use part of his emergency money. On top of every hill he cuts the motor. Lets the car coast down. It groans and shakes.

We barely make it to Aachensee. We kids spill out on a strip of the shore and stare dumbly at the dark trees forming a green shawl around the clear alpine lake. Sheer rock rises here and there high enough to touch the sky. Patches of snow wink from mountain tops. We totter around like old folks, our legs and arms are cramped from riding so long stacked into that old car like cord wood.

But what picturesque scenery. No rubble anywhere. After we come back to life, we can't believe that nature here looks so unscathed. It's almost as if no war happened. And as if there won't ever be another one. That's a strange feeling—to think there could be a world without war.

None of us older kids has ever gotten over that deep fear that another war is inevitable. Peace is the abnormal state for us. Peace and quiet is odd. That's borne out by our parents' constant fighting.

It's rubbed off on us and we start fussing: What's to eat?

With a shrug Vati heads into the woods, leaving us kids to fend for ourselves. So here we go again. We check out the blades of grass. They're tasty, all right. And maybe we can find some juicy wild flowers we can boil. Or wild onions or berries will beckon us. Encouraged we look around this beautiful crystal-blue lake surrounded by pines growing in ant- and chigger-infested soil. If they can make it, so can we.

Sure. Things look up. Isn't there always hope? Hope and hunger being the best of friends.

A nice campground with a metal waterspout for drinking water stretches nearby. Of course, we don't have the money to camp there. So we set up camp outside the grounds. At night we can always sneak in over there and steal their water. Maybe treasure-hunt in the trash of the other campers who look well fed. Always a good sign.

Bound to find something.

That evening Vati comes back with some meal that he mixes with water, then cooks over a fire. From then on, once a day for weeks we get a chunk of "bread" that tastes like wood shavings but fills our stomachs. A little. The problem is what it does to our digestion.

Which is nothing. Our process of elimination has shut down. Totally.

So even though we strain every three or four days as we squat in the woods, it's a week before our system processes the saw-dust bread. Then comes the real emergency.

Our waste, what little there is, is rock hard and gets stuck in the place where it ought to come out. And we groan from the various strategic places deep in the woods where we crouch for hours. We're pushing and pressing down. Do whatever we can, but what we're trying to eliminate just isn't budging. It's plugging us up like a cork that won't come out. So in despair we have to take little sticks, sharpen them and start digging at our backsides. Trying to make headway there.

No, not hard. Easy, easy, be careful. Don't make a mistake and stab the cheeks, puncture your butt, injure yourself bad.

Slowly, slowly we dig out dark pellets. It takes

hours, hours when you're crouching and poking yourself in the back. And sweating and groaning for dear life. There's blood, and the rock-hard pellets finally emerging look like what animals leave behind. The little boys cry, of course. I help them as best I can. Help get their plugs out.

One good thing: After you get some of the black rocks out, at least you can stand up again. Whew. But you sure never want another bite of the dry mealy bread. Yet it's all the food we have.

And how long can you chew on weeds and pine needles? We've already done that for so many years. So Ger and I start looking for other food sources.

There have to be some morsels in this paradise.

We wander down to the end of the nice camp where people quickly cover their food as we pass. Hide it from us, that starving horde. Be that way, we say, hurt. We don't want any of your *Scheisse*. Later we strike up a conversation with a cheerful little man. He runs the camp store, a kiosk that sells the bare necessities and is attached to a hostel that's empty at the moment. The people who have rented it for the summer haven't arrived yet.

Ger and I offer to sweep the store and the man nods. Sure, go right ahead.

We do the most meticulous job, even throw in dusting and mopping, window washing, raking up pine needles around the store, for free. I'm good at those things, thanks to Julie.

The storekeeper watches us, his eyebrows going up. The smile never leaves his face.

Keep it up, girls. Hit the basement next. Who

knows, I might let you have a couple slices of bread.

Real bread?

Sure.

We furiously clean the whole hostel, which has dozens of small rooms with cots and mattresses. And the basement. The man throws in some rancid margarine with the stale bread. Wow. How quickly the little brothers stop crying when we show up with "real bread and butter" that evening.

Problem solved. We will not die on this vacation.

From then on, Ger and I do all the work for the happy little man, and in no time he turns the whole store over to us. This is what you do. When the customers ask for rolls, hand them over. Put the money in this drawer. Got it? If they want a liter of milk, dip out three ladles into their pitchers. Understand? Three. Three. From the big can into their container. Put the money in the drawer and don't cheat me. I hate cheaters. So don't even think about it. *Versteht ihr?*

We understand perfectly.

From then on, all he does is count his profits, but we munch on real bread and butter every night. Sometimes he lets us have an apple, which we cut up and share too. *Wunderbar.*

Soon the man lets us run the store by ourselves, and Ger and I love it. Business increases. Ger and I are friendly. Lots of people start stopping by from all the campgrounds around Aachensee. They're happy when they see us but always grumble when they leave. It's the milk every time. Ger and I taste it, but it's fresh. The dairy farmer who drops off the big full can every morning isn't to blame.

Still any customer who buys milk leaves muttering, and we don't know why.

Until one day when some campers from France pull in and hand us an empty bottle with lines. A liter of milk, *s'il vous plait*. Ger dips out three ladles with her prettiest smile, hands over the milk—

You damn *boche*, the French customer says, shaking the bottle. You damn German swine. First you start the war, take over Paris. Destroy our works of art. Bridges. Ruin our country, and now this?

Ger and I are stunned. What's wrong?

That's only three-quarters of a liter, damn cheaters. It takes four ladles to make a liter! You Jew murderers. Pigs, bastards. Think because you're young gals in skimpy outfits and grin, you can cheat the hell out of us? *Mon Dieu*, but we'll get you. Defeat you again, sue you—

Fists are raised. The woman's screaming attracts other campers. They fly at us, yank our hair. More tourists come running, visitors from England and America too. All those folks we've been cheating for days and days and others. Screams assail us from all sides in several languages. But the message is clear: We want our money back, you filthy murdering Germans you. Trash. Bastards. Slimy criminals.

It turns into a riot. Ger and I have to fight back. She's fearless, bashes everyone in reach with the milk ladle. Red-faced I hand over cash, hot rolls, all the milk anybody wants to pacify the screaming customers.

The happy little man hides under the counter until the noise dies down, then fries us an egg each.

You *dummkopfs*, he says. How could you? What's wrong with you fools?...But I have pity, you just made a damn mistake. Well, what can I do? He slides the eggs on plates, sets them in front of us.

Ger shoves the egg plate back at him: I quit. From now on you can do your own damn cheating.

I quit too, I say reluctantly. My fried egg looks heavenly. And besides, how will we feed the little brothers now? The big ones are clever. They know how to steal something here and there. Know how to show up at the moment other campers eat supper and get themselves invited. But the little boys just sit naked in the mud all day and pee. On their backsides rashes bloom. Their bony little arms and legs are covered with pus-filled welts. They need some good food.

Ger storms off, but I linger, eyeing my egg. And hers.

C'mon, stay on the job. I've forgiven you already, the little man says. Sighs. You sure drive a hard bargain. How about if I let you sleep in the hostel tonight?

You mean it? This isn't just another trick? Another way to cheat somebody?

Oh no.

I run to find Ger. He's going to give us a room from now on. What do you say?

A real room? she asks.

Sure, a room for you two, the happy little man says. For as long as you want. Of course, that means you also have to run into town, starting today. On foot. Takes an hour either way. Tote back my supplies. But yes, sure. You can sleep in the hostel. Naturally, take all the sheets off. Wash them by hand.

Hang them up, dry them. Iron them. Mend them. Piddly things like that, but yes. You get your own room just as long as you wish. Damn, you gals are blood suckers.

It's beginning to rain. Hard. We accept. Gladly. But from now on everyone who buys milk gets four overflowing ladles full, plus some. And we undercharge folks as much as we can. Ha! And we luxuriate in our own small room. Just two of us, Ger and me, in a rustic, musty little room the size of a closet with the beams showing. What deluxe accommodations. We sleep on cots with lumpy mattresses, our sheets smelling of sunshine.

It's turning out to be a real vacation, our first one ever.

A week later in the middle of the night, there's a terrible commotion downstairs. Beams of light flare up from numerous flashlights. We peek out the window. A big bus has pulled in the parking lot by the hostel and a boys' school from Le Havre, France, is unloading. Dozens of teenage boys swarm into the hostel and stake out their bedrooms.

Ger and I lock the door. This is our room. We're working for it, we paid for it. There's a pounding. Get out, you damn squatters. It's the little man who acts as if he's never seen us before. How dare you sneak in here? German pigs, cheaters, Jew killers. First you overrun Austria, annex the hell out of us. Now this shit, he yells. *Raus, raus, raus.* Or I break the damn door down. Have you sluts arrested.

Ger and I are wearing nothing but our shirts, pull on underpants still wet from washing, grab our skirts.

Try to get down the steps past the boisterous French boys. They laugh and scream. Whistle and hoot. Oo-lala, girls, girls in our beds, German girls—

No, don't look at them. They're trash, the lowest of the low, their leaders say, priests, in rapid French, which we don't understand. But we can tell what they mean from their looks of horror. Then they repeat everything in broken German for our benefit. This is a Catholic high school on their annual camping trip, and we're damn *boche*, German swine, nasty, filthy pigs, sows, whores. Stinking, dirty, bad, evil. Murderers, Jew killers.

But the boys get more excited the more the priests curse us out, try to grab us, pull us into their rooms, touch our hair. The priests start chasing us, their cassocks flapping. They punch us, shove us. Out, out, you sluts.

I'm 12. Ger is 13. We don't even have boyfriends yet.

It's long after midnight when we run to our ragged tent, huddling pitifully in the darkness. We look inside, in the slice of light the moon allows. There's not an inch of space left. Only wall to wall little brothers, and outside by the meager ashes curl the older brothers and Vati. All are snoring and making other body noises. Some of the boys are groping around in their sleep like dogs searching for a bone, and the three youngest wake up: We're so hungry. What did you bring us?

Nothing. Ger and I slump down on the dirt by the lake. Look across it. The lights are out everywhere. Calm has finally descended back at the hostel too. All

GERMAN SWINE

people have a place to sleep. Everyone on earth, except us. The night is dark and still except for the concert of farts of the big brothers and the whining of the little ones. I lean against a tree. Ger scoots next to me, falls asleep with her head on my shoulder. Her breathing brushes my chin, my neck. I let her sleep, stay awake all night thinking. Why?

In the morning, a deep-peach light streaks up behind the Alps and paints the sheer rocks in color. I feel a thread of hope in me, a tiny flame of promise. Maybe, maybe. Maybe life won't always be so hard.

I'm just dozing off when I hear: Oo-lala. It's those French boys again. Early risers. They have tracked us down, found us. Hound us from then on. Ger and I can't make a move or go anywhere. There's always two or three jumping out from a bush. They talk to us, hey you, *boche* girls, the war's over. *N'est-ce pas?* Really, you're not to blame. You can't help you're swine. We want peace with you, real bad. We a new generation. *Oui? Oui?*

This is a new world.

But the priests eye us with hate, promise the boys eternal damnation if they don't stay away from us, treat us German kids like lepers. Every time the French boys talk to us, they have to kneel down for hours afterwards and pray for their sins.

Still the boys pursue us when they aren't building intricate altars with elaborate wooden ornaments. They hammer together make-shift benches in a clearing in the woods. Here the priests say mass several times a day. Mostly they pray for deliverance from us.

We watch, often from our various vantage points

in the woods. We're having to keep digging out what's impacted in our innards again. Spend hours trying to dislodge the black pebbles that refuse to come out on their own.

The priests, dressed in gold and purple silk sashes, bless the clearing and the woods. When they step into something that stinks, they stop outraged but only briefly. Then their voices get more beseeching. Deliver us from those Huns, oh Lord. Please. Soon a big revival is to be held in this very place, and the pace of all the preparations keeps picking up.

When the bishops and all the other religious dignitaries finally arrive for the revival, the altar is gone, the crosses too. My brothers have dismantled everything for fire wood. Naturally the smaller sticks are being put to good use—to dig out their backsides.

A last gigantic volley of screams comes in our direction: Dirty filthy heathen *boche* swine, scum of the earth. Then buses pull up, motors are revved. The dignitaries race to their limousines, which whisk them off. All vehicles speed away. Obviously the priests fear everlasting harm may come to their boys if they're around us another second.

We tell Vati that we overheard the priests announce that he and his band of wild kids will rot in hell.

He grins: Great. I prefer it down there. That's where all the interesting people will be, in hell where it's nice and warm. And cozy. You never have to worry about getting any firewood there. Up in heaven it's ice cold. Brrr. Worse than any Bavarian winter. And who wants to wear nightgowns and fly around with big wings? Huh? And have to sing the same pious boring songs over and over anyway?

Ger and I desperately want to go to heaven. Please God, forgive Vati for talking like this. But we keep quiet.

The following year we're back at the same campground. The store owner's already waiting for Ger and me and again lets us stay in the hostel until the people who've rented it for the summer show up.

This time we keep all our clothes on, sleep in coats near the backdoor. So we can scram whenever someone will show up, no matter what time of night.

It's midnight again. And just as we feared, it's more parochial schoolboys from France, freshly washed in starched school uniforms, their hair neat, their faces rested. Not a sign of malnutrition on them. Look at those many teeth. They're all straight and even. White.

Hurriedly we sneak out the backdoor before the boys can corner us. But this is an entirely new bunch, so not to worry. These boys are all carrying thick feather pillows that they've brought with them all the way from their homes back in Le Havre, France.

After they have settled in, we ask one of the older boys who speaks German: What's with those pillows?

Oh, you *boche* girls, he says, don't worry. We know you didn't kill the Jews. But don't you know? We have to pray even harder now every time we talk to you girls after the riot you caused last year. You're getting older and prettier. Oo-lala. So the priests have threatened us already. Stay away from the German pigs. And kneeling on the hard ground's no fun, so we brought along these pillows. In preparation.

Because we plan to have some serious praying to do this summer, *mon Dieu!* That's for damn sure.

CHAPTER 12

Lungs of Glue

My next job pays money. Fifteen cents an hour. *Wunderbar.* What happened was that by then, the early '50s, Germany is not only rising out of the ashes again, but it's really on the go. *Vorwaerts*—forwards. Pumped up by the Marshall Plan cash infusion, the wounded country has scabbed over and is healing fast. The scorched-earth look is replaced everywhere by frantic rebuilding. Vast spaces are cleared in towns and cities, fresh walls shoot up, stone cubes break out of the earth and multiply. Shimmering bridges grow and span across the rivers again. Small shuttered shops take a deep breath, burst open, and swell into gigantic stores with immense glass fronts. Roads are patched, craters filled with rubble and paved over for parking lots. Armies of shiny Volkswagens, Mercedes-Benzes, and BMWs march off the assembly lines and zoom along the repaired Autobahns in all directions.

And no longer are the farmers king. Educated city folks are in demand again. People with learning leap ahead. So in no time Vati is hired by the Opelwerke in Ruesselsheim am Main, a town not far from Frankfurt.

Before the war, he had worked for himself in his own successful business and has trouble taking a low-level position. Like he always reminds us, the war broke his spine, though he stands up straight. But now at least, he has a professional job again, even though it's far below his capabilities. But what a thrill it is the first time he brings home not a day laborer's paycheck but twice that much.

I remember how he cashes it and hands over all the money to Julie, who's been waiting impatiently for this great day. Julie sighs. In anticipation, she's already spent the money months ago. But now at least she can charge more food at the grocery stores that let her charge the sacks of potatoes and flour needed to feed all of us. Or maybe she can buy some new material and finally sew herself a new skirt and kerchief. So when she goes to scout out yet another grocery store farther and farther afield where nobody knows her yet as the wife of Dr. Hans Vierling, the brilliant and good-looking inventor with 11 hungry and wild kids, she won't look so desperate and have no trouble getting credit.

But from the first big paycheck, Vati keeps two more crisp 10-mark notes.

My *real* emergency *gelt*, he says. That's it. Never to be used except in the most extreme case, understand? Only in case the world ends. He folds the bills like rare parchment and tucks them into his shabby billfold, which he pokes out of sight. Now we won't ever starve again. At the first sign of the next world war, we'll buy plenty of seed, plant a garden and grow vegetables.

Potatoes. The little boys clap their hands.

Cabbage

Carrots

Tomatoes

Cucumbers

Green beans

Any kind of beans

Food, food, food—Mmm.

Cherry trees, the older brothers say, their cheeks grimy but round. Even though we can now buy a few groceries, they still haven't switched over from their preferred way of getting something to eat, stealing. Here in Ruesselsheim, they start by raiding other people's gardens.

Many an afternoon, they steal what they can from the orchards in the area and stuff themselves until they're sick. But the orchard owners catch on eventually and from then on, there's frequently an angry ringing at our front door. When I open the door, an irate man or woman yells at me:

Where are those damn thieves? Where? Out with them. I'm calling the police.

I don't know what're you talking about, I say.

Those damn boys. Punks stole all my plums, pears, strawberries—whatever's in season. Didn't leave anything.

But, *Entschuldigung.* There are no boys here, only girls.

But I saw them run into this house.

Are you sure? I say and make an innocent gesture. The wonderful thing is that on the main street in Ruesselsheim where we now live, all the houses look identical. There are rows and rows of gray one-family houses on both sides of the street. Company homes, built for the men toiling in the Opelworks. Everyone around for blocks works for the same firm, and every house has the same front door, the same tiny yard, and houses a family. So how can the poor ripped-off folks ever be sure they've come to the right place?

All I have to do is wait, stand my ground, look angelic and deny ever having seen any thieving boys....

Of course, as soon as the angry man or woman leaves, I go find my brothers and demand some of the loot. The little boys are hungry.

So it's working out just great. The Hessians love gardening even more than the Bavarians. There are always more neat vegetable plots and greenhouses to clean out. More fertile fields to forage in. More orchards with plum and pear trees to plunder....

Then Vati starts bringing home flowers. I'm thrilled. Maybe the new job and the new environment has doused the open hatred between him and Julie and rekindled some affection. Not that I want another little brother. Heaven forbid. But one day of blessed silence would be wonderful.

Julie throws the flowers on the counter. Don't you know what that means? she says, sewing new curtains. She's not even bothering to run through the litany of names, not even checking if there's someone in the room with her or not. He's got a new girlfriend, damn that bastard. Ouch. She's stuck herself with the needle.

I arrange the flowers in a vase, back out of the room. Track Vati down. Easy. He's set up another cellar workshop with all his favorite junkyard scraps, nails, screws, hammers, pliers, bits and pieces of rusty metal and pipes. Where did you get those flowers?

I told the boys to get me some.

Why?

I thought Julie would enjoy them.

She hates them.

At least I tried.

You know what she thinks?

Perched on a homemade stool, he's chewing the end of a pencil and staring at the slide rule, holding court on a crowded table in front of him. What?

That you have some...other...woman....I'm waiting for him to deny it outraged. Hoping he'll burst out with: Are you crazy? Me mixed up with another woman? You must be insane! All I want is to work on my inventions. My life's work. Understand? My *raison d'être*. Now get the hell out of here!

Vati bites through the pencil. Look what you made me do? Dammit. Thank goodness he's angry. I shouldn't have asked him. Julie's crazy, I know it. She'll say anything to make Vati look bad. And what's the matter with me anyhow? None of my brothers and sisters seem to care about the flowers. They just survive. Shrug and live. One day at a time, one meal after the other. Sleep, eat, be. Why do I always have to stick my nose into things?

Vati meticulously glues the pencil back together, affixes exact strips of tape to the outside. Now what? he growls when he sees me still standing by the door. Then he remembers what I came for, clears his throat and says, I deserve some credit, you know.

Yes, of course. It was nice of you to bring her flowers. I'm sure once she thinks about it, she'll appreciate—

He interrupts. Let's just face it, OK? Most other men can only go two years. I can go five....

I wait.

...With the same woman, that is. All other men I know stay in love with one woman for only two years. But I always make my loves last five years.

I don't know what to say to that.

After that, he goes on, no matter how hard I try, a wife's just like a sibling to me. The romance is gone. Kaput. She's a sister to me....Are you old enough to understand that?

I shake my head and my face burns as if he had slapped me. Did you feel the same about my Mutti? I whisper.

Oh, her. Her....Hmm....He takes his time thinking back. Well, she was different, not at all like Julie who always goes against what I tell her. Barbara did whatever I told her. Exactly. But you must understand the great difference between us. She had little formal education. Poor thing. He gives a chuckle. One time before the war, we hosted a big dinner party for all my business associates. I wanted to finalize a major deal. Even my mother came. Anyway, the conversation turns to foreign languages. Out of the blue Barbara announces she can "speak Latin." *Lanu*, she trills and points at the moon. *Lanu*. Everybody laughed, everybody. Was I ever embarrassed. These were all university grads from the finest of families. My mother was so upset she had to leave the room.... He looks at me, waiting for a reaction.

I bite my lip, thinking that this would be funny if it weren't about my Mutti. I know what she was trying to say: *Luna* is Latin for *moon*, not *lanu*. Mutti was always examining the sky at night.

Vati seems disappointed he doesn't get a rise out of me and goes on: Let's face it. Barbara just wasn't smart. At all. And was she jealous. *Gott!* I couldn't even peek at another woman. I think it was she who tipped off the Nazis that I wasn't in the army. The next day they came and escorted me away. I'm not absolutely sure it was she but....Of course sooner or later they would've come for me anyway. But that was right at the beginning of my work. I had it then. The first electrical automobile. You know, that crucial time when you first crack a puzzle? When you can envision it *all*? The glorious moment of breakthrough?...I never even had time to jot down the steps. So I lost it and it set me back for years. Even now....Ever since, all I've done is try to reconstruct what I invented back then. Listen to me, that woman, she wasn't smart at all—

I don't want to hear any more. Stop running her down. That was my Mutti, and she's dead. I slam the door behind me.

Upstairs Julie is still furiously sewing curtains.

Pinpricks all over her arms sport drops of blood....

So it's just not working out, it seems, our new life in Ruesselsheim, even though Vati makes money now and the boys have a good thing going with those numerous gardens. Most haven't been cleaned out once. And there are so many more in the direction of Frankfurt. By the time the boys will have hit all of them, the year will be over. Then they can start in our vicinity again.

I plan to sew them a bag, tell them: Fill it to the brim. Or else I won't cover for you ever again.

But it's just not working out, no matter how hard I try. Which is too bad, for the kids are all doing fine. No one's been arrested yet. But it's the adults; they are getting worse. The flat landscape, the absence of the Alps, the sameness of the houses all highlight the wrath between them. Instead of the passing years healing Vati and Julie, like Germany's healing, they have tons of landmines buried in their marrow. So anything can set them off. Their fighting escalates; the name-calling and the blaming each other get worse.

And worse.

But why? We have plenty of potatoes now, cook them with the stalks of green onions and mash them into mountains. I serve everyone Alps of food. We eat delicious bloodwurst too on special days. Tripe dripping with gravy. It's delicious if you breathe through your mouth only and chew and swallow fast. On extra special days, we fold slices of bread around pork rinds and eat them with ox tail soup. Of course, we boil the same ox tail over and over. There's always a little more flavor left in it. *Ausgezeichnet!*

But nothing the other kids and I do can stop the screeching, no matter how fast I jump to my chores, how many mouth-watering meals we girls stir up. Vati and Julie still don't stop fighting. It's always over *gelt*.

Every morning there's screaming that wakes us up. Don't need an alarm clock at our house. Outbursts erupt like sudden storms and continue in the evening when Vati comes home. They last deep into the night. Pillows over our heads, cotton stuffed in our ears, staying out late ourselves—nothing prevents us from overhearing the intense fights.

So we have to sneak into the house after school, become invisible, do our chores silently. Whatever you do, don't let Julie see you. When she does, she turns on us: He's terrible. That man is the worst failure, I'm so disappointed in that bastard, calls himself Dr. Hans Vierling. Finest family, shit! Damn broke fool, what a weakling, *Flasche*, pervert. All his great inventions, just idle talk. Nothing but *Scheisse*, brings in nothing. Asshole. Already spent 20 years on his great idea. And for what? And always more kids. Always trying to get me pregnant again. To hell with him. That son of a bitch, sex fiend, maniac—

In the evening during the few minutes Julie takes to catch her breath, Vati takes us aside: Don't listen to her ravings. She's crazy, *verrueckt*! You know that, don't you? She's always been crazy, loony, batty. Out of her damn mind. Sick, sick, sick. Jesus. And what a big spender, show-off, fake. Never enough for her no matter how hard I work in that damn plant. Lower myself, kiss ass. Does she appreciate it? No. Nothing but a damn nag, a pure wastrel. So extravagant, never has enough. Always wants to spend more and more. Nobody's running around naked. Has anybody starved yet? So what the hell does she want? What's her damn problem? He sucks in air, starts again: Wish I could lounge around all day like she does. I could do my life's real work then, but no. Every day I have to go to that stupid Opel place. And nothing but screeching when I come home! Females, damn disgusting uteruses. That's what they are. Nietzsche was right when he said, when you visit women, don't forget the damn whip! Jesus Christ!

He balls up his hands, and we kids flatten ourselves against the walls and want to disappear. Inch away without being noticed. We let the screams blow over and around us like ill winds, just waiting for a lull, a good moment to make our escape. We become polished liars. Sorry. Gotta go, check with the neighbors' kids about school. Lost my sweater, look for it. Run to see if there's a sale on potatoes. Isn't that one of the little brothers crying in the yard? Sure. Let me just run and see....We say anything to escape from that hell house. Run, run, even if you forget your shoes, just tear down the street, fast. Far away as you can.

Hurts always seeing Vati and Julie go at each other so relentlessly. Hurts every time no matter how often we kids hear the same yelling. But there's no calming either of them down. Unless somebody in the family makes some extra money. More money might help. I decide the money maker has to be me, the middle child. Five kids are older than me, five younger. And none of them do anything except mutter and curse. They all can't wait to grow up fast, get out of this insane asylum, fly the coop. Be gone.

But deep inside I know I'll never get away. Never. The aprons Julie makes me wear are my shackles, my handcuffs. Maybe the older girls could leave. Yes, sure, they could escape but not me. The little boys depend too much on me. So I need to go to work. Now. But what work is there for me, a scrawny ugly 12-year-old girl with big buck teeth and running sores on her skinny arms and legs and a sad thin face? Black craters under her eyes? And with a permanent frown?

Fortunately we move back to Bavaria, this time to Munich. The BMW plant there offers Vati a better-paying job. But the new street where we live in a small duplex with all of us crammed into three bedrooms and one small bathroom, with no hot water—Balanstrasse—has possibilities. There's a low-slung building across the street down a block that's a brush factory.

It doesn't look like a horror factory from the outside.

❦ ❦ ❦

Inside is a different story. In the large dim hut that seems to stretch for half a mile, rows of old women hunch over tables piled high with brush-making materials. A moving band runs along the edge, where they deposit their finished products.

The women's faces are wrinkled and look caved in. Their mouths are thin-lipped slits. They have hardly any teeth left, and their matted hair is tucked under black kerchiefs. Their small eyes look dipped in iodine and skip around viciously. In reality these women are no more than 30 or 40, but years of hard labor have aged them prematurely.

They talk nonstop about men's body parts, one in particular. And the more graphic their descriptions, the more everyone cackles. His was *this* big, let me tell you. But all bark, no bite. Never could stay hard.

Bigger than a salami?

Way bigger. More like a whole bologna sausage, but mushy like liver pudding, no matter how I worked on it....

While the women talk, their mottled hands are separate creatures. They dart like lizards from one task to another—from piles of bristles, which first have to be separated into small bundles, then cut and tied together, to the flat wooden handles, which have to be painted red or green, polished and filed down at one end, to the metal sleeves, which have to be stuck on the filed-down end of the handles. The hands move so fast that soon the pile in the middle of the table shrinks and more materials are deposited there while their handiwork moves along the assembly line from left to right. Every woman works feverishly. Nobody slows down the process.

Until the end of the moving band, where chaos reigns. There a mountain of work is piling up, and every few seconds more appears and adds to the disaster.

The foreman leads me to the huge pile-up. Sit down right here, he says.

I do, feeling the women's eyes fasten on me. It's like getting pelted with gravel. Even though I wear my usual rags and have my hair tied up like they do, I'm taller than they are due to my colt-like legs. All those forced marches through the woods at the Ammersee have straightened my legs. Made them long and slim. But everything else about me is pathetic. My eyes are too large for my thin face, my teeth are in terrible shape, and I look worse than the women. Still they hate me on sight, maybe because the foreman pulls out a chair for me, then takes a minute to show me what to do. Grab some bristles, stick them in the glue, stick the glue end into the metal sleeve, way down, and then nail—Where's that damn glue at?

The women point outside, where pots of the worst-smelling goo sit fermenting in the sun. Cursing, the man hefts in a dozen heavy cans, shoves them under my nose. Get started, will you? What's your problem, gal? You got a lot of catching up to do.

I can see that. Thank you, I say, but just barely. The smell of the glue has filled my nostrils and traveled up my nose making me instantly nauseous. No wonder the women moved the glue outside. And no wonder they have left this job for me. I start retching as the women laugh. Meanwhile I'm trying hard to do what I've been told—grab the bristles, dip them into that awful glue, poke them into the metal sleeve attached to one of the hundreds of handles. Find a little nail to pound into one side, another nail into the other....

But I spill the glue and the nails get sticky. And the bristles won't fit into the sleeve because the glue is drying too fast and anything it touches sticks together for eternity.

Anyway, I'm so sick by then that bile boils up from my stomach into my mouth. I haven't eaten any breakfast, but does my stupid stomach care? No, it just pools whatever stomach juices it can muster up and shoots them up again and again. Into my mouth. I swallow the bitter-tasting stuff back down, while trying to see what mess my clumsy hands are making. Still haven't finished a single brush, yet more and more brush parts keep piling up to my left. The women cackle louder. Finally they see I'm hopeless and go back to talking about men's sausages again, what kind they like best. What you do with them....

By then I have trouble breathing. Am choking. The vile glue smell has penetrated every cell of me. And it isn't just in my hair and face, which happened when I tried to wipe my nose which started running out of protest, but it's managed to seep into every pore. From there into my organs. My lungs are screaming. Air, air, give us some air. But I can't stop what I'm doing. Can't give up, I'm too determined to learn this damn job. My family's survival depends on it. And if those women can do it, so can I. Never mind that they have all the easy work.

I turn my head sideways, hoping to catch a whiff of fresh air coming in from an open window, hold my breath as I stick bristles into the glue and ram them down a sleeve, nail in the tiny nails—quick, quick—

By then I almost pass out, but the first brush is done. I elbow it aside and come up for another whiff of fresh air. Then again: right hand grabs bristles, dip in glue; left hand has brush handle poised with metal sleeve ready. Ram in those dripping bristles, position nail 1 into place. Hammer twice. Turn over brush. Nail 2 gets pounded in—

More fresh air, please. God. While my stomach keeps roiling, spews bitterness up my throat. My lungs hurt worse than anything I can imagine. Tears flood my face but I keep on, gritting my teeth. The women glance at me, see my despair, laugh louder, but still I don't give up. I'm a robot. Work, work, work.

It's disgusting.

After some time my hands begin to know what to do on their own. It's as if they realize this is a matter of life and death. I can only hold my breath for that long and if they aren't quick enough, I'll faint. So they hurry up and start darting around like the mottled hands of those old women. And on and on it goes, that terrible nightmare. More and more work marches toward me from the left. More and more and more brush parts. But little by little I begin to make a dent in the big pile. At least it's not growing any more. Maybe if I whittle away at it a little every day, I can reduce it over the next few days....

If I can only make it through today, this first awful tough day. By now my body has begun to accept the fact that I'm not leaving and I'm continuing to hang on to consciousness. More bile shoots into my mouth, yes. But I just suppress it again. *Nein, nein.* I'm not giving up.

The minutes pass like years. My whole body aches. I'm weak from the effort of holding my breath for so long, only to snap up a little breathable air every 30 seconds and even that air is glue-tinged. Now there's nothing about me that doesn't stink of that awful glue. I have dripped it on my rags. Droplets have pasted themselves on my arms and the back of my hands. They also speckle my ankles and what's visible of my legs. And my hair is stuck together from all the glue drips flying when I have to turn my head fast for air while my poor hands already grope blindly for the next pack of bristles. The bristles sting like dozens of needle pricks. Glue seeps into the prick wounds and burns, but all that is nothing compared to my lungs, which keep protesting against that evil smell. They scream. Scream for mercy.

I can picture my lungs filling with millions of invisible glue droplets and caking up, thus losing their capacity to breathe. Sure, that's it. This job will ruin my health. I'll die in a few months, surely. And the pain in my chest gets worse and worse as the hours pass slowly. So slowly. The women pull out a sandwich, share it as they work. Pass around something to drink too. I have brought nothing and get nothing. Good thing—whatever I would eat and drink would only come shooting up again, I'm that sick.

Oh, I can't do this any longer. Stop that moving band! I see flashes of light in front of my eyes, but nothing stops. On and on, it goes, that ribbon that delivers more work to me. There's no second to catch your breath. No rest, only unrelenting work. It seems as if I've been glued to this horrible table for centuries when finally, finally, finally a whistle blows.

The women hop up, gather their pocketbooks and rush out. I stand feebly with only the greatest effort. Have to hold on to the table. Take a tottering step, feel like I've been gassed. Every organ hurts. I can hardly see and what I see is obscured by dancing black specks. A few wobbly steps—but I made it, didn't I? Yes, dammit. I made it. My relief is so overwhelming. I really did make it through my first day of work. I breathe out as hard as I can, maybe I'll get some of the glue fumes out.

I can do this horrible job. I did do it, one whole day already.

By now the women are all gone. I drag myself out of the factory, one step in front of the other, every muscle in me screams, every bone aches.

My lungs are the worst. They don't know what to do now. After inhaling putrid glue smells for so long, they can finally have all the fresh air they want. So I breathe in and out fast, like a runner. I pant, pant. It feels like I'm breathing fresh oxygen, but still my lungs can't believe the torture's over and they ache, ache. But slowly the pain's ebbing off, ebbing off....

Finally I drag myself home. It's not far to my house but it seems many miles. I have aged so much in one day but am glad I lived through it. Don't the elms along Balanstrasse look pretty as they reach for the blue sky dotted with white puffs of clouds? Aren't the Mercedes cars and BMWs whooshing past on the street shiny and brand new? Buses filled with workers lumber past and I feel a bond with them: We are the workers of the new Germany. The rebuilders.

The houses with their red tile roofs greet me like someone who's come home after a long absence—like a prisoner of war released from a Siberian concentration camp. I know how those broken men look, act, feel. My uncle Heinz is one of them, a poor broken man with his health ruined. I feel just like him.

Finally I drag myself to our house, shuffle into the kitchen where Julie is boiling a bone in gallons of greasy water. The scum floating on top is dirty like snow that's been hanging around too long.

I made it, I say. Really. I did, I lasted the whole day. Oh, was it terrible. This job is the worst. But tomorrow is going to be much easier.

Straightening up all the way for the first time is painful but I try. Until then I walked like a woman crippled with osteoporosis. Now I muster my last bit of energy and stand up, all the way up. My lungs still hurt but one good night's rest will restore them, surely, though I'm afraid they'll never be healthy young lungs again. Oh well.

Julie stares at me. What a sight I must be with those bristle bits stuck all over me and glue splotches on my ragged clothes, face and arms. And red and green paint flecks on me. Just look, she says.

I know I'm a mess, I say. But you have no idea how plain awful it was—

No. Just look at the clock. Julie looks thin and gray and drawn. Her eyes are vacant, as if she's given up hope as she turns back to that bone bobbing in the scummy water.

So I look at the clock. Blink and blink. It's only 10 AM. Turns out the whistle blow was only for the morning break—15 minutes—which the old women used to run to a bar, toss back some Lowenbrau or schnapps. Smoke a cigarette or two....

When I trudge back into the huge hut, late and heartbroken, they're laughing again. In my absence they piled up another huge mountain of bristles and brush handles, and I sink back into my torture seat, my lungs screaming in protest.

❦ ❦ ❦

How I long for school to start again, be like other kids, have time to run outside, oh just suck in a few normal breaths of air. Fortunately once school starts again, I'll only have time to work a few hours in the brush factory and not those killer days anymore. Maybe then I won't have to worry about spitting up blood anymore either....

But school is so far away. This is just the start of summer, and my family counts on the money I bring home on Fridays. Julie's always waiting for me at the gate then, her worn hand out.

I give her all my money, hoping for September.

So time creeps again. It's like those slow gray years of hunger in Bavaria. Now it's the torture years in Munich. They're just as slow and gray. Meanwhile the city is rising again fast. It's a new shining fortress. But all I ever see is the inside of our home where housework is waiting, the inside of school, where I pretend to be dumb so I won't get singled out, be called to the front of the room, expose the back of my skirt to scrutiny. Once one of my teachers says to me after class: You know, you don't have to carry the burden of the whole world.

I stare straight ahead, bite my tongue so I won't say anything. What I want to say is: Sure would be nice if that's all I had to carry. Only that one thing, the burden of the world, that wouldn't be bad. But no, I have to carry that plus so much more—my family, plus the guilt of my whole country. Plus the burden of injustice. Plus whatever else I'm subjected to.

Like those forced hikes again. Now that we're back in Bavaria, Vati makes us hike dozens of kilometers again on the weekends when it would be so nice to sleep a little. So nice to catch my breath just once.

Up, up, it is again, early on Saturday mornings. And the hikes are even more strenuous now. Munich is farther away from our old trekking grounds, so it takes longer to get there. Much longer.

At first the boys refuse to cooperate, but Vati coerces them. All he has to do is separate them, give them a beating when he has them alone. They fall into line after hearing from one of their own how bad the beating was.

So we set out again, Vati and his motley crew of kids, still starved, still wearing shoes that hurt. But it's different now. We don't like digging in trash piles so much anymore. Refuse to shake down the apple trees we pass on the way.

You're getting damn spoiled, Vati says. You know that?

True. We sure don't like to snuggle into big piles of hay anymore, couldn't care less about spending the night in a barn. Hate raking together all the wet grass we can to make our pallets. A piece of dry bread just doesn't taste as good as it used to. We still eat it, but without the thrill it used to give us.

And nobody offers to carry a little brother now. Vati is on his own. Those are his brats, let him tote them.

We've become grumpy. Bad. Real bad. When Vati

isn't looking, the older boys pull out slingshots, kill birds, squirrels, whatever else they can but not to eat, just to let some meanness out. Just to kill.

When we pass a pond, one of the big boys picks up a rock, but doesn't make it skip across the clear water like he would have years ago. Those were the games back then. Now he looks for a frog, throws the rock hard as he can. Hits the frog. Good shot. But at the moment the frog falls, Vati turns around.

Stops in his tracks, comes charging back to where we kids are. What have you done? he screams. He picks up the frog, starts massaging its belly, bends his head down. Blows air into the frog's mouth. Little puffs of air, puff, puff. Keeps massaging the frog frantically.

In seconds a frog leg jerks, then another. The little green body twitches, the yellow belly rises, falls. Vati puts the frog down. It hops away slowly, then faster.

Vati screams again: See there? If I hadn't revived it, that poor animal would be dead. What's the matter with you? With all of you? What are you, a bunch of killers? Haven't you learned anything from history? From going to church? From school? From me? Life is sacred, *mein Gott!* How could you do this? How could you? He stares at us, eyes wild. After what we've seen in this country! The war, all those innocent people....On and on he goes....

I know it's coming, the one thing I've been waiting for. Finally, finally. Vati will tell us all about Dachau. He will say either that he didn't know about the Jews getting killed there and is sorry. Or that he did know and is sorry. A man who has such compassion for a little frog must have compassion for human life. I lean closer to him, can't wait to hear what he has to say—

A shout from one of the boys: Shut up! They stand so closely together that it's not clear who said it. Now Vati is even more enraged. How dare anyone of you tell me to shut up? Who was it? Who?

The boys shrug. They're not telling, and Ger and I are too shocked to say anything. Until now nobody's ever dared to talk back to Vati who launches into another tirade. Then the sky opens up. Rain gusts drench us, and we don't even try to stay dry.

On the way home, we walk in the middle of the street. All of us are completely soaked to the skin. When Vati strikes up one of his many folk songs, he's the only one singing. The little kids try to hum along, but I'm silent. Why didn't I speak up when I had a chance? That was my opportunity to mention Dachau. Ask once and for all what Vati knew or didn't know. What he did or didn't do. Ask him. But I didn't ask. Coward. *Feigling.*

The rain is a warm shower but I shiver. The boys box each other as they walk, smirk. They're like, what can he do when we gang up on him together? Not much longer now, another year or two, then we'll tell him where to go.

Show him in person. *Arschloch!*

I feel the growing tension in them, worry that the next time he rants at them, takes one of them aside and beats him, they'll stand up to him. Slap him back. And then a fight will ensue that won't end until one of them is wounded.

I sure have an ominous feeling about where this is leading to. Feel goosebumps popping up all over me under the warm rain shower that's been reduced to a trickle.

Oh yes, there's trouble ahead, big trouble. I can sense it. The day my brothers will refuse to knuckle under, when they will stand up to Vati and hit back, someone's going to get hurt. Hurt bad.

Or worse will happen. A tragedy. A big family tragedy.

I'm right.

There is a big family tragedy ahead for us.

But I'm wrong about whom it will involve.

CHAPTER 13

Tunnel of Tongue

Whan people who survived the Holocaust era meet, they always regale one another about their hardships as children. Poverty, starvation and living through years of a terrible war, with bombs lighting up the night sky and slews of relatives getting killed make for great stories. Nobody likes to have had it easy during those years. It's a badge of honor to have lived the most miserable life and suffered the most.

It's one-upmanship at its best: You starved for six months? Hey, we starved for six years.

You ate handfuls of dirt? We didn't even have any dirt to eat. We had to gnaw on chunks of rubble.

All I ever say is: Show me your real teeth.

It's always the teeth that tell the truth. For if as a child you starved a little or moderately, you'll have a few bad teeth, some ugly and a few missing. And if you starved more severely and for a longer time, you'll have half your teeth gone by age 40.

And if you starved for years and years, and on good days subsisted on only weeds, bark, nettles and yes, dirt, then you'll hardly have a tooth left by the time you're grown.

The fact is, a childhood of abject poverty can be painted over later by nice clothes. You can stuff yourself later in life, plump up proudly and bulge over your belt. And a lack of education is simple to overcome. Books are bountiful. Bury your nose in them. Living in rubble also is quickly forgotten once you have bought yourself a nice rancher.

And to make up for losing your family you can substitute your own kids. Discover traits in them that remind you of your lost ones. Water those traits and curry them until your kids play the parts of your dead sisters, brothers, parents too.

And for the deep sadness that comes from never having had a childhood you compensate by feeling great joy at everyday things—sunshine, a tree in bloom, taking a big breath—and seeing life as a smorgasbord.

But lengthy severe starvation, malnutrition and rickets always, always exact a steep price—and that price is human teeth.

🐛 🐛 🐛

My teeth were never right from the moment I had my first ones. The loss of three babies within two years—my sister's twin, my twin, and little Ingeborg, born a year after me—was such a blow to my mother that she didn't recover physically and psychologically, so her milk dried up. She hired a wet nurse to feed Ger. But that was in 1938, before the war started. By the time I was born, no such luxury existed. I was fed on watery milk or just water sweetened with saccharine tablets. Little sugar was available. Then of course, the years of real starvation started and with them came the rickets-scurvy-trench mouth.

My teeth didn't get enough calcium from the start. Later they loosened and started moving around in my gums. I remember one year when they were all jiggling in my mouth. Years later they settled into my gums any way they wanted. Some crooked, some sideways, some spaced apart. The front ones protruded severely.

No problem. We were such a large family with more important things on our minds, such as how to get enough money together to have something to eat at least once a day....

The strain of that constant struggle finally breaks Julie. She packs her boys, not only those from her first marriage but also those she's had with Vati and goes back home to Cologne. There she sticks the boys in an orphanage in Bad Honnef and goes to work.

Vati is stunned and stops inventing for a moment. Although he's watched Julie lose control more and more, he can't believe there's so much fight left in her. How can she rally?

Immediately he begs her to come back, promises to reform. There's no divorce allowed in Catholic Bavaria, so that's out. Anyway, what in hell is he supposed to do with his own four kids? Just at a time when he's *this* close to another scientific breakthrough!

Plus he misses the little boys who're still too young to question him, to disobey. They are still his disciples, wake from their starved stupor when he comes home, like we used to before we got to be older than 10. They run to him, look up to him like a god.

But we older kids are getting contrary, and this separation does nothing to placate us. For no matter how relieved we are at the silence settling over our house, we know it's only temporary. Vati and Julie can't live without fighting with each other. The war has turned them into warriors. Aging warriors who want to spar, duke it out with each other, forever and ever.

So how long will it be before they reunite?

Not long. That's a fact. We know that this is just the calm before the cyclone.

The reason: Vati is powerful like a force of nature. He can walk into any room, and a bright light comes on. One look at you and the rest of the world fades away. We children have never had enough attention from him, never had more than a few moments with Vati. Yet we know firsthand of the steel in his gray eyes and the brilliance behind them. He will get Julie back, one way or another. That's why he takes that job at the Opelworks in Ruesselsheim, where the older boys will soon clean out all the orchards.

So as expected, the peace and quiet don't last long, and soon we're all together again; only it's worse here in Hesse. This isn't Bavaria. There are no clear lakes, no Alps. There's only that lazy Main River with oil streaks from the tugboats that drag on like our days, slowly and without color.

But somebody there notices my grotesque teeth and after many consultations the dental clinic at the University of Mainz is persuaded to take me on as a charity patient.

I come home from school one day, ready to arm myself with my hated apron and kneel on the floor to scrub the kitchen and other rooms, then attack the usual mountains of stinking sheets and underpants with cold water, a sliver of harsh hand soap. Julie stops me in the hall.

I just don't know whether I can trust you, she says softly.

What do you mean? I'm sullen. Don't waste my time, please. I got too much to do as it is. The sun's shining and I'm a prisoner—

Don't you remember? Today's the day you've got to see that dentist in Mainz.

No, I don't, I say. At almost 13, I've never been to the dentist before. I don't want to go, but she makes me, although she keeps hesitating. I just don't know whether I can trust you....

With what?

This money. She shows me a 20-mark bill (worth five dollars at the time), the only money she has until the end of the month, not enough to feed one person that long, and certainly not a family with so many kids.

It's all I have, she goes on. You need it for the bus. Those damn social workers sent a train ticket to Mainz for you, but no bus fare. And this is really all I have. Here, take it but don't you squander one penny of it. Not one....

I hang my head. I know I can't be trusted with money. Whenever I have some, I give it to the man without legs at the corner. Or the blind woman. *Gott!* Just last week I had 25 pfennigs for another bus ride. As I was getting ready to board the bus, I saw a little boy with his face pressed against the window of a bakery. He looked scabby with snot running down to his little chin. He had on ragged pants, a thin shirt, no shoes and looked like he hadn't eaten all day. I hopped off the bus and bought him a *krapfen* (jelly-filled donut). That meant I had no bus money and had to walk home six kilometers in shoes handed down from my brothers that are stuffed with folded newspapers. See? I do waste good money. Julie reminds me of it. And I've done it before. Many times. I'm just dumb, never think of what I'm doing.

Julie stares at me. But this time, child….She doesn't remember my name but knows I have to show up at that dental appointment….This time, promise me, on your life, you won't waste any money. It's truly all I have. Promise me, promise me.

I promise.

And don't you lose it either. Here. She tucks the bill into a small purse. So remember. Don't dare spend any extra, or let anyone take it from you. If you do, just don't come back. Ever. Do…you…hear …me…?

I hear you.

I fling the apron aside, run to the station. Maybe for once somebody else will do my chores. Maybe Julie will do them. What a relief that would be. I don't care how bad the dentist's visit will be. At least I don't have to wash all those stinking clothes, hang them up. Ha! Feeling good, I clutch the purse to my chest. Nobody, but nobody will get this money. They'll have to kill me first.

Anyway, I'm free. Free for one afternoon. Free as a wood thrush. I hum two notes, my favorite ones, over and over. Those that mean "Pay dirt. Paradise."

The train pulls in almost empty. I find a window seat and settle in. The wooden benches are molded and hard. Feel comfortable to me. Leftover magazines wink at me—free stuff to read. I scoop up a bunch. Movie magazines, depicting Hollywood faces and figures. Fantastic. One small magazine is a Christian Youth pamphlet with Jesus on the cover. It was stuck between the movie magazines; that's why it ends up on my lap. I shove it aside.

Start flipping through the movie magazines, feeling on top of the world. What a break: I get to read about some famous stars without Julie's interference. Once in a while I glance at my reflection in the window of the moving train, pretend to be a movie star too and smile. But always quickly close my mouth again. My teeth are that horrible, even to me. Don't I know I'm ugly, have always been and will be?

But anyway. I'm on my way to have something done about those teeth, and I'm holding the little purse tight. Nobody can get it, even as I look at all the movie magazines. Nobody would dare. I'd kill them. Simple as that.

At the next station a mild-mannered, middle-aged man enters my compartment, sits down across from me. He looks at me and I duck behind my magazines.

Ha! If he thinks he can get my money he's crazy. I clutch my purse tighter.

I give a small smile, bury myself in reading about Hollywood. What a life.

Then the man clears his throat, starts talking to me.

Pah! Is that how he's trying to get my money? I wonder. Is he going to be chatty and when I let my guard down, he's going to snatch my purse? Have I got news for you, *Mensch*.

I lay the magazines aside. Use both arms now to clutch my little bag. I'll bite him if he makes a move toward my money, I decide, and clench my teeth in preparation. But the man is nice. Neat brown hair, calm eyes, shaved and clean shirt. He moves closer only to inspect the magazines I put down, fishes out the Christian Youth pamphlet and says: What a joy to see that young people today still care about Christ.

Hmm, I go. I have no trouble with Christ, but I'm bothered about all the money in the hands of the church when we don't ever have enough food on the table. And where was the church when Dachau happened? Hmm, I go again, softly this time.

That must mean you're really a fine young girl, he says.

Hmm—hardly audible. I feel bad because I'm not what the man thinks I am. And I should tell him so. What I should say is: No, I'm not a fine young girl, I'm a nervous, ugly, mean young girl who has no intention to read that Jesus pamphlet. But I don't.

He goes on: How nice to see you're such a good good girl.

Hah! I know what's up. He's just trying to get me

talking. I can sense it. He's just buttering me up, so I'll let down my guard. Relax a little. Then he'll steal my money. Grab it and run off. But *verdammt!*, is he wrong. I'm way too smart to fall for that, now holding my pocketbook just as tight as I can.

When he keeps complimenting me on reading the Jesus pamphlet, my hmm's fizzle out. Maybe now he'll leave me alone.

But the man is crafty. Tries another tactic. You see, other kids your age wouldn't have any use for a Jesus pamphlet, he says. They'd spend their time reading about all that filth in Hollywood. He points to the big glossy publications. But no, not you. You're pure and innocent. On top of that, you're *so* pretty....

Whoa. Now I know I have to speak up. Admit I read the movie magazines too. Set him straight once and for all. But I'm concentrating so hard on clutching my little purse. And deep inside I'm glad to hear what he's saying. Not that stuff about being pure and innocent. Garbage. But the part about me being pretty. Which is an outright lie of course. I'm ugly, so ugly.

Hmm, I say, louder again. Because it does feel good being called pretty. Feels like a spotlight is turned on me. My face burns. Makes no sense, as bad as I look, but I am vain. I admit it. Still, I wish we'd get to Mainz. Hurry up, train. Hurry up. Because I'm uncomfortable in the presence of this man who's grinning. Silly old fool. Seems to think he's found a way to get to me. Obviously he assumes nobody ever called me pretty before. And my flaming face proves he's right.

But so what? He doesn't know whom he's dealing

with. While I can't control my blushing, I'm not about to let go of my money, no matter how often he says I'm pretty. On the contrary, I clutch the purse tighter. Tighter. Hurry up, train.

Already there are signs outside announcing it's only a few more kilometers to downtown Mainz. Just a stretch of a tunnel. Then one more short stop and then—

Not that I would blame you if you did read a movie magazine. The man again, making me focus on him again instead of what I can see through the window—the small towns on the outskirts of Mainz. Because you're actually prettier than all those trashy starlets, he adds.

Now I'm truly on to him. Aha. He's giving it one last shot, idiot. A film has broken out on his forehead, and his eyes wake up, dart around. I guess he's thinking hard of what outrageous lies he can ply me with next. Wants to make sure my mind is spinning with all his lies. Then he'll snatch my purse.

But I'm not relaxing a whit, even though my neck is burning along with my face. My shoulders feel cramped. Then I freeze all over. Suddenly I know what his game plan is. The tunnel. Oh no. The tunnel—that's when he'll make his move.

The train is about to enter a long tunnel that leads to Mainz, and I steel myself as darkness floods the compartment. The light dims and dims until I can only see the man's outline. But I'm more keenly alert than ever. Watching his every move. I'm the lynx again, the animal-like crippled baby I was years ago. When all I did was watch and listen as the bombs ruled the sky and people whispered: London.

The Amis.

Die Juden.

I'm taut like a spring. My mouth opens so I'm ready for the exact moment when the man's arms advance towards me.

For I'm going to bite him, hard as I can. Chomp down.

Oh, oh, here it comes. Here it is, the deepest part of the tunnel, and what I'm dreading, the man's making a move. But I'm right. The man has been waiting for this. He's beginning to move. Gets up, comes toward me. I feel like screaming, but who would hear me? The train surging through the tunnel rattles loudly. I decide to stick with my plan, to bite into whatever part of this fool I can sink my teeth in. What I'd rather do is box his face, his shoulders. Attack his chest with my fists. Pummel him with all my strength. Beat the *Scheisse* out of him. Growing up with so many brothers taught me how to defend myself. But I don't have my arms free. They're a vise around my little purse. So I have only my legs. But the man's so close now, his legs press against mine and immobilize them. So my legs are useless.

He leans over me. Any moment I expect to feel his big fingers on me, pinching and yanking my purse away from me. But he won't have any luck. No way. I stretch my neck, snap at him and try to grab any part of him with my teeth. Clamp down. But instead of pulling back, the man comes still closer. His face is ghostly in the dark. I feel his lips press on mine. They feel slimy and swollen.

Stunned, I shudder and forget about biting him. But I'm more determined than ever not to release my purse. Even when his thick tongue enters my mouth and forces itself down my throat, I hold on tight to the money. I hold on.

But the man's very tricky. Has yet to reach for my purse. Instead, he keeps pressing himself on me, and his tongue makes me gag. I can smell his odor. It's sweaty and stale, like old vinegar. Makes me sick and I want to hop up and run away. But his weight pushing against me paralyzes me almost as much as my fear that he'll reach out and grab my purse. Yank it from me as I'm running away from him.

So I stay put, hang onto my purse for dear life. Meanwhile I suffer from the big tongue that makes me gag and retch. Oh, I pray for the tunnel to end before my strength gives out. Please, please, please....

When lights again flood the compartment, I shake my head vigorously. Start twisting and thrashing to the left and right until the man pulls back with a sound of pain. I tear myself away from his big hands that have begun to grope me before they can snatch my purse. Quick, quick, I hop up. Run. Must get away from that thief. I race toward the exit, past all the other benches. There are other people sitting not too far away who glance at me as I'm tearing past them, both my arms still clutching the little pocketbook against my breast.

I'm scared out of my mind that the man is following me. Don't dare look back. By now he'll have realized his mistake. He didn't grab the money when he could have, that complete *Arschloch*. I keep chasing through the compartment and the next and the next to the front of the train, which is slowing down. Last stop before Mainz! But never mind. I hop off and start running through the station, outside, along the sidewalk. Away, fast, faster. Faster than I've ever run. My heart's beating wildly. I feel sick to my stomach, want to throw up.

Several kilometers down the road I stop out of breath and finally dare to look over my shoulder. There's no sign of that slimy thief. Thank God. There are just people. Gray war widows in mink-collared coats walking their dachshunds. Young women with bouncing brown hair buying red cabbage and bunches of marigolds at the open-air market. Pretty young mothers carrying packages of *Knackwurst* in their yellow nylon-net bags. Little kids rolling rainbow-colored marbles in a vacant lot swept clean of rubble. Girls and boys my age screeching over their badminton games. Oh, just life as usual in the outskirts of Mainz. A Mainz that's been rebuilt, so gleaming new structures blend seamlessly with old war ruins.

I lean against a glass and steel apartment tower, spit on the pavement. Try to bring everything up that's in my stomach. Want to get that taste of the slimy fat tongue out of my mouth. Between spitting and clearing my throat, I keep checking my little purse. But no, don't worry. The money's untouched, it's right there, all of it, he didn't get it. Whew. This time I was smart with money, wasn't I? I'm proud of myself but sick at the same time. When I finally walk to the Dental School in Mainz it's after hours. The place is closed.

But Julie is glad when I get back home: This time you didn't waste any money, not one *pfennig*. Not even for bus fare. It's all here.

I don't tell her or anyone else what happened. What's there to say?

It was all my fault that I got *this* close to being robbed. My fault for letting that strange man talk to me. Heap all those stupid lies on me. Which I should've stopped. But for a second I so wanted to believe that I was pretty, and he instinctively knew my weakness.

He could tell I'm vain, which I am. Ugly and vain, the worst combination. And he was almost able to rob me.

But how did he know there was money in my purse?

I can't figure that one out and deep down wish I could tell someone about my triumph. For I out-smarted that guy, didn't I? Probably made his ugly tongue bleed. Wish I could have kicked him where it hurts.

But there's no one to discuss this episode with. All my brothers and sisters are too busy just surviving. And too busy being bitter spectators. We see the German economy flex its muscles again. We watch wealth wake up. Everyone has good jobs shortly. Streets are newly paved, and houses multiply. Overnight, war reminders are removed, razed, stuccoed over.

The new *Wirtschaftswunder* gilds the land.

But instead of life getting better for us during the '50s too, it only gets worse. As we children grow up, we want more, need more, but get less than ever before. That puts everyone in a bad mood. Except for Julie. Suddenly she acts as if she's forgotten all about our family situation, Vati's modest income. Sure he has a respectable job title now—inventing engineer. He's that brilliant and handsome Dr. Hans Vierling again, the man who was the smartest kid in school in Weiden. When he started first grade at age four, he was so little he sat on the schoolmaster's lap. Every morning when he strutted to class carrying a huge book, the merchants in town said: Here he comes, our little scholar. Our child genius. Right on the dot as always. Guess it's time to open our stores.

Oh, the stories they used to tell about Vati. It warms my heart to hear them, but it scares me too, because I know he's not what he was back then.

Far from it. So far.

And Julie?

Julie is worse too, underneath. Inside. Like the new *Wirtschaftswunder* generation, she's simply wiped a whole decade from her mind. Gone. Never talks about the war, about how hard it was for us to live through it. What Hitler did. And the Nazis.

And what the people let them do.

Instead, she laughs a lot now and skips from new bank to new bank borrowing money. It's an unparalleled economic boom time. And money is easily available. Just ask. She does. References are seldom checked. And Julie, still wearing her one formerly good suit that's now freshly dry-cleaned, is able to impress lots of high-ranking bankers, loan officers, money lenders.

But the war happened. The Holocaust happened. Her first husband has been killed. Her brother lost an arm. Her mother lost her mind and walks around showing her lavender underwear to strangers. Her 11 children suffer from severe malnutrition. Worse—her personal war, the one between herself and my father —has never stopped. Not once. It only escalates.

By the time I'm a teenager, Vati and Julie are arch enemies.

Their biggest bone of contention?

She wants a house of her own too, a new one, whitewashed walls, new furniture, refrigerator, dammit, like all the other *Wirtschaftswunder* wives are getting. Wants it now. Is going to get it no matter what the cost. And every child in her reach is going to help her get her dream.

Meanwhile Vati hasn't changed a bit. He is still the obsessed inventor, his head in the clouds. The man knows innumerable theories but has no common sense. And the older Vati gets, the more he's con-sumed by an urgency to work on his inventions, especially his most important one, the first electric car he designed in a closet in the Fliegerhorst Koethen, when he was forced to become a soldier for the Nazis. When he hid whenever he could during the daily Heil Hitler pep rallies and sketched out his ideas, calculated degrees, angles. All the numbers were right there.

The finest of fine points, the most brilliant ideas. The essence of his creativity.

One moment he had it.

Then he lost it. Lost it all.

When the Nazis broke his spine.
But it's more than that.

CHAPTER 14

Hollywood in Bavaria

Some of my classmates sense how poor we are, how desperately I need money, but they don't have enough money themselves to give me some. Or they don't know how to do that. It's awkward to tuck cash into a girlfriend's pockets. But they do care and constantly try to help out by pointing out opportunities to me. Where I might get another job. Where I could get some extra cash.

Lucky you, you're just what they need, they tell me one day during the 10-minute break we have in school, the St. Anna Gymnasium, on the St. Anna Platz where the beautiful St. Anna Church is, whose back pews will never be the same.

By then I've mastered my periods. *Gasthause*s have *Rollen* of toilet paper now. So I always have plenty of tissue. My girlfriends don't know the reason I'm more outgoing now is that I don't bleed through my clothes anymore. They crowd around me, never mentioning the fact that I'm wearing my one outfit yet again. Inside I know they're counting: How many days can she go wearing that same old skirt and blouse?

What're you talking about? I ask when they keep prattling about a new way for me to make money.

The movies. You ought to be in 'em.

That's crazy. Hollywood's in America. It's a zillion million miles away. And I look dreadful.

No. You don't.

Thanks.

Anyway, Hollywood has come here. To Geisel-gasteig. That's on the outskirts of Munich. A movie studio has just announced that they're looking for extras. Bound to pay more than the brush factory. The maid work you do all the time. C'mon, wake up.

How do you know?

Here. One of my girlfriends pulls out a newspaper clipping: Auditions tomorrow morning, 9 AM sharp. Out at the newly renovated studios.

Why don't you go there yourselves?

No, this is for you. It's fate. See, right here? They're looking for tall slim girls that have that real post-war look, but fine features. You know, somebody who looks haunted, starved, abused. Just like you.

Thanks a lot.

No, we mean it. You have just what they want. Former nobility that's bitten the dust, OK? Could be they're making one of those post-war films. From war girl to *Wunder* woman. Could be an easy way for you to grab some cash. Really.

Wouldn't Julie rejoice if I came home with a bundle?

Well, sounds interesting but I can't go, we got school.

Nothing to it. After the break, just tell our teacher.

Jaja, right. I'm going to tell her I want to try out for one of those movie extra jobs and she's going to excuse me from school tomorrow?

No, just pretend you're sick this afternoon. Good practice for the acting job. Then she won't be surprised when you're absent tomorrow....

❦ ❦ ❦

On the way home I check out the streetcar schedule that goes to Geiselgasteig. Figure out it will take me 45 minutes to get there. First walk 15 minutes to the stop, then that 25-minute ride, then walk five minutes to the studio.

It's possible. I have enough change for once, but have to leave the house by 8:15 AM at the latest.

Can hardly sleep that night. Up early the next morning. But two of the little boys threw up during the night. So it takes extra time getting them ready for school. Scrub them, find them some clean underwear. And of course Julie's sitting in the dark kitchen, stone faced, no breakfast for anyone.

So I have to run next door to a neighbor. Beg for some bread, lie, scrape.

You never admit we have nothing in the house. That's not done, so you make up a story. It's our mother's birthday. So we're letting her sleep late and want to make a special breakfast for her, but we forgot about it until the last minute. Could we borrow some oatmeal?

The woman frowns, gives me a cupful.

And some milk please?

What're you gonna do? Rob me blind?

No, please, just this once.

Ach. What about all the other times you've come here and begged and never paid me back once?

Oh, I'm sorry. I am going to pay you back. In cash. Very soon. I'm going to make some extra money today....

Run back into our kitchen, fix the whimpering boys something to eat. Look at the clock.

8:25 AM. My God. Where has the time gone? I take off running. Traffic is bumper to bumper on Balanstrasse. I can't get across. Finally dart between the speeding cars. Then I'm on that kilometer-long avenue, at the end of which the streetcar stop is.

I run, but can already tell I'll never make it. Feel tears collect in my eyes. Damn. Run down the side-walk, gallop, lunge forward. It's impossible though, a futile attempt. Forget it. Still I keep racing along on the sidewalk, praying, anyway.

A car stops close by, a delivery truck. The driver backs up, rolls his window down

Trying to catch the 8:30 streetcar?

Yes. I keep running,

He drives along beside me, cheerfully. You'll never make it.

Idiot. I don't bother answering him

Hop in, *Fraeulein,* he says. I'll give you a ride.

Oh thank God. What a lifesaver. I collapse onto the passenger side of the truck and the driver takes off. A small man, dark-brown hair, brown eyes, more cheerful than before, whistling. I'll get you there, no sweat. Don't you worry, even if I have to stop at a traffic light.

He does, but then zooms ahead: Where you off to anyway this morning?

Geiselgasteig

I see. Trying to get in the movies, huh?

No, I just want to be an extra. Make a little money.

Don't blame you. He eyes me. Reckon you're just what they're looking for. I know. Ever since they opened the studio back up after the war, I've seen girls flock out there. Some made it big.

Another light, but it has mercy on me. Changes fast and, we're moving again, only a third of a kilometer now, then less, when I see the streetcar pulling in ahead of us

Hurry, hurry.

He slows down: Relax. I'll get you there. This truck goes faster than any streetcar. I can always catch up with it at the next stop. So don't worry.

Oh, thank you for your kindness, I say. Let my breath out. Straighten my hair. My heart beat is slowing down. This is turning out well after all. I'll make it to the studio in time, I think when Plunk! the man's left hand lets go of the steering wheel, reaches across toward me and lands on my breast.

What're you doing? I ask horrified. Edging away. The car is moving. I can't jump out, and even if I could, I could never catch up with the streetcar now.

Just getting a little feel.

Take your hand off, I say. Right now. I try to brush the meaty hand off like a gross insect that's landed on me. But he grabs me, squeezes me. Won't let go. I'm angry, enraged. What do you think you're doing?

In the few seconds it takes to get hold of the man's fingers, bend them back, push his hand off me for good, I have a flash of Vati and me. When I was 12 and we were back in Ruesselsheim, on the lower bunk bed every late afternoon his smooching started. First a hug and a kiss on the cheek, then it escalated. A kiss on my lips, two, three, then all over my face, then down on my neck. Hugs turning into a vise. I feel heat, feel beloved, feel cozy, special. But not for long. I really don't like this. I'm not comfortable. This is wrong.

One day I say, I don't want to do that anymore. No more!

Without realizing it, I've been punching the stranger. Stop. Stop. Pull over. Let me out. Now.

Why? he says, unperturbed by my punches. All I want is a feel, dammit, nothing else. Look here. I'll drive you out to the studio, drop you off at the front door, pick you up afterwards—

I said, pull over. Right now.

Finally he does, shaking his head. What's the matter with you? Huh? Why did you get in my truck in the first place? He lets me out, cursing; peels off, tires screeching, and I turn around. Walk home. Julie doesn't move when I enter the kitchen.

In school the next day, a classmate says, I was there. Hey, they were looking for someone just like you. Showed them your picture. Where were you? What happened?

I couldn't make it.

Too bad, she explains. They ended up picking

some girl from another school not half as pretty as you.

❦ ❦ ❦

Another chance a year later. Or more correctly, another teasing from fate.

Someone famous from America is arriving in Munich. He's in the military. By then I have been chosen to spend a whole day at the American High School. No money involved. This is just to foster German-American understanding.

The American school building is a brick cube and the grounds are unimpressive, but inside the rooms are full of laughter. Full of fun. The kids, about my age, wear the most beautiful clothes. The fabrics are thick, brilliant-colored. The girls have swinging ponytails and bouncing skirts from under which lacy layers peek. Small waists are cinched together with pretty leather belts. White socks and shoes that tie complete their outfits. The boys wear snowy shirts, rolled up at the sleeves, tight khakis, shoes similar to the girls'. All their clothes are brand new.

The committee in charge of the visit finds something likable in me.

I bet he'd like to meet you, they say, referring to the famous person while eyeing me up and down.

Why? I ask, my thoughts on all the work awaiting me on Balanstrasse.

He just wants to meet some young German girls.

What does he do?

Now he's in the army.

No. What did he do before he entered the army?

Drove a truck.

I'm silent, and they think I don't know that word. Truck, they explain. You know, a big car, a van, do you understand? He was a driver, back in America, before he became so famous. He drove around.

Thank you, I say. But I'm not interested in meeting this truck driver.

They scream: Are you crazy? You don't want to meet Elvis Presley?

CHAPTER 15

Embryo Brother

One good thing about being back in Munich is that Vati's making progress with his invention again. So he's in a great mood these days, which makes him talkative. Want to know the damn truth? he says one day, chuckling. Julie and I are now at the age where we're both just waiting for the other one to die first. Happens with a lot of older couples.

He's 50; Julie is 40. Then he's 52, 54. And she's 42, 44. And still the same old line.

It makes me shiver but whenever Julie hears about it, she just says: Won't be me. It's going to be him, ha ha. But the ha ha is hollow.

We children, meanwhile, are mostly mud. Stick to whatever parent we're with at the moment. *Jaja, sicher, richtig!* Right, we say and wait for the inevitable—a major clash between them. World War III. We sense their anger, hate. All their misery is boiling up. We don't know what to do about it but sure don't want to be around when it happens.

It's going to happen. Can't be swept under the rug much longer like Dachau.

So the mud starts oozing out: The older kids flee just as soon as they can. Rats leaping off a torpedoed ship, they hurry, hurry. Out, away, *raus*. Let's get out of here before there's an explosion.

Heda, the oldest, manages to get accepted into a fine, private, all-girls boarding school, with money my grandmother contributes to "save at least one of the children." Good for Heda. She's gone in the blink of an eye. And when she comes home on infrequent visits she is a changed person, taller, freer. She flows. Tells us of meeting all kinds of nice boys, of going to dances with the son of Baron von Kronin, the youngest brother of Count Rotzky, the cousin of Earl zu Schmitterhausen.

Oma beams. Oh, oh. Her society has taken Heda in with open arms. Finally there's someone who brings honor to the family again. Back to the way we were!

From then on Heda spends much time with Vati's brother and sisters and their kids. Those are the *real* Vierlings.

I say *Scheisse*. We dirty kids stuck in this terrible house are the real Vierlings.

Fact is, however, we have many relatives that we're rarely in contact with. They're all ashamed of us, but Heda is welcome in their circle. All she has to do is pretend she's an only child. Her parents were killed in the war. Nice and clean. That's it, easy.

That story makes her much more likable and isn't a total lie. Mutti did die in 1945, and Vati's as good as dead. Inside anyway. And Julie can't wait for his outside to follow suit.

And we other kids are trash, especially me.

Except I'm trash that's curious. *I want to know.*

So I ask Heda when I can get her alone: What have you learned in that high-society school?

Lots. For example. She clears her throat and counts, using her callus-clear pink fingers. One. You can't ever go wrong wearing a tailored suit. It's a great look for afternoons and evenings. Change to a fancier blouse is all you do. Really, it's so easy to have class. Style. But two, don't ever forget the main thing, little sister.

Which is what?

Gloves. See here? Made these myself. She waves maroon kid gloves in my face. They look good enough to eat, but I restrain myself. Don't nibble, only sniff at them.

Not about that, I say.

I get it. OK, three. About meeting the right kind of boys. That's easy too. Just think back to what we were before the war. Remember our big house in East Germany? Our maid? Our *Kinder maedchen*?

No.

That's right, *Mäuschen*. You were born at the start of the comedown, the ruin. Poor thing, little lynx. It's easier for me. I just act like a *real* German. Like nothing bad ever happened, see? Don't tell anyone, but I only talk about how it used to be before the war. Then I tell about those nuns in Diessen. Now I'm in this fine school. A good bath, shampoo, fashionable haircut. And that suit I was telling you about. The gloves. The boys. That's it. Nobody can tell the difference between me and the other girls. I get invited everywhere, meet their brothers. Of course I study, make A's. You have no idea how easy it is to make all A's if that's the only damn thing you got to worry about.

Very interesting, I say. But what about *it*?

What *it*?

You know…Dachau?

Mein Gott! After all these years. Are you still hung up on that?

Yes, always. For as long as I live.

Oh my, my. She pats my arm, sighs. Nobody talks about that. Shit. School here is just like the public school. The history classes, I mean. At the beginning of the year we start out with the ancient Greeks and Romans. Follow them through the centuries. You know the drill. We study the Goths and Franks too, the Anglo-Saxons and so on. By the time we get to the 20th century it's always the end of May. Or early June. We always cover World War I. Every year we go over it in detail. Then we get to the late 1920's, and voilà. The school year's over. Tada.

I'm disappointed. Same in my school. I have never had a single one of my teachers touch the 1930s or even say Hitler's name. Not once. Even our history books stop with the early 1930s.

So it goes, Heda says. Pulls the gloves on, a perfect fit. Her hands look rich. Made them myself without a pattern. Meanwhile a little red spot sits on her cheekbones. I guess the teachers are all ashamed, she says. They probably keep the new history books under lock and key.

You think that's it? They're ashamed about not doing anything about the Holocaust?

Jaja, sure. Or ashamed about not knowing anything about it.

How could they not know anything about it?

I don't know. Guess they were all so damn scared they didn't want to know. Last week when I went over to Aunt Hedi's for supper, I found out she was a member of the *Hitler Jugend*.

No! Really? Vati's little sister was a Nazi? Oh my God.

Yes, but listen. She was only 15 at the time. Still she spent time in jail after the war.

For what?

She had to get de-Nazified.

What's that?

Heda laughs. Guess it was punishment for being pro-Nazi.

I take a deep breath. Now tell me the truth, was Vati ever for the Nazis?

No, never ever.

But did he know? I bounce up and down from impatience. Did he? Did he?

Hold still, will you? Heda says. Calm down. That's not acting like a lady. She grabs my shoulder, sighs. I really don't know. I have never asked him.

Heda! Never?…Not once?

No, I was always too scared. What if he didn't know? That would make him so damn stupid, and he's a genius, isn't he? Supposedly? So I don't want to know, all right? A look of pain washes over her face. And honestly, if Vati did know, then he's a disgusting criminal. And I definitely don't want to know that. So stop it, Eri, just stop it! Stop asking all these idiotic questions. How many more times do I have to tell you that? Just stop it.

Heda is agitated now. The little red spots on her cheekbones have blossomed into dark-red flowers, matching the color of her gloves.

OK. OK, I say. But just one more question, please, Heda, please. Please. The last question I'll ever ask you.

She closes her eyes, nods, and I say: What about our cousins?

Oh, you mean Aunt Toni's two boys? She smiles. Poor fellows. They were drafted, both of them. At 13 and 14 they had to join some other skinny little kids and march against the enemy. Ridiculous, wasn't it? They didn't even know how to hold a gun.

Then what?

Then they got caught by some black Amis. Can you believe it? Scared those boys out of their mind, seeing some black people for the very first time. Anyway, those black Amis were real nice. Took their guns away, gave them some chewing gum. *Kinder*, they said, go home to Mama. *Schnell, schnell*. And that was that.

So there never were any *real* Nazis in our family? Never ever?

No, not a one.

I let my breath out. But why doesn't that make me feel any better, Heda?

Because you're such a damn *Dummkopf*, she fusses.

You enjoy being miserable. Why don't you forget all about the past and study hard? Impress Oma? Maybe she'll rescue you too, send you to a nice private—?

Nein, nein. I don't want a damn *pfennig* from her. No, never. Oma was mean to my Mutti.

❦ ❦ ❦

See you, Ger says with a smile as she dashes out of the house. *Wiedersehn.* My middle sister is so talented she is able to snare a scholarship to an art school in Augsburg. Overnight she moves out too, with her high heels and pretty belts, and not just out of the house, but out of town. How convenient. She comes home even more seldom than Heda.

And when she does, she beams. She's been showered with praise by her instructors and wears it like an armor. Her wild flower paintings are alive and bursting with color.

Now Ger's cheeks are round and soft again. Her blue eyes look untroubled. Her forehead is smooth, dewy. Her old clothes, with a smidgen of oil paint here and there, make her look like a real artist. New belts sparkle around her slim waist. She has a boyfriend who talks about himself all the time. So she's not ever having to talk about her own sick background. Lucky her.

And the older boys top even Ger. They don't wait for some great opportunity. Just drop out of school en masse and get jobs that either require them to be gone for weeks of traveling, lucky dogs, or give them a chance to leave the country entirely.

Australia is looking for immigrants, they say as they wave bye-bye. God, it's good to get out. Escape.

But I, the intense, buck-toothed girl with stick legs and hollow eyes who never smiles, am not smart or talented. And I can't just leave. There's only one girl left in the house now: Me. So my absence would ruin Julie totally.

I can do nothing except stay where I am, go to school where I daydream, make average grades, and work hard at all kinds of jobs after school and during the summers to make some money.

And as the only chump left, I serve as first-rate whipping post. That means I get all the abuse heaped on me that occurs when parents declare an all-out war against each other. I'm the lightning rod.

Plus, of course, the maid and babysitter for what's left of the family, which is still plenty big. There are always the five boys younger than I to look after. Always five brothers to scrape up enough money for. Also shop for, cook for, get their clothes washed, darned and ironed. Get them off to school, help them with their homework....

Oh, there's a world of work to do and nobody does anything but me.

When I get a free moment, I lock myself in my bedroom, try to think. But even that doesn't work. There's always someone pounding on the front door. Someone wants payment for a bill Julie's forgotten about. Or someone else complains about what the boys did to his yard. Or it's the electric company again, wondering why our bill is so low. Vati's tapping into the power line down the street, so we have hardly a bill at all, but it's tricky. I must remind him to let us run up some small amount so we won't get caught.

And another time it's a strange thin man: Is Dr. Hans Vierling in?

No, he won't be in until later.

What time?

After seven. But then he's got lots of work to do in his—

Oh. Is he still working on the big one?

The what?

His big incredible new invention? The one he started before the war?

Yes, I think so, I say, surprised that the stranger knows so much about Vati. Have you known him that long?

Sure, I've known him from way back, the strange man says. Dr. Vierling always treated me just like family, you see. Really, he's the nicest man I ever met. Shared everything with me. That's why when I couldn't stand it any more I came directly here. I need a job and just hope he'll help me find one.

I'm sure he'll do his best. Please come back tonight. It would be one evening without the constant screaming since Vati and Julie always know when to keep quiet. They don't fight in front of company. It's just not done. Where did you come from? I ask.

Israel. I didn't like it there. And I always remembered how very kind your father was....

❧ ❧ ❧

When Vati comes home, I corner him, describe the man and ask: Who is he?

Just a former neighbor. I lost track of him after the war started.

Will you help him?

What a question. Of course, I will.

I gather up my courage. Is he a Jew?

You don't have to whisper. Not anymore. Really. Of course, he is a Jew. What do you think? What's the damn problem?

But isn't it odd that he should come back here? After all that...trouble—? But I'm excited. Finally, finally we're talking about *it*.

Vati shrugs. I guess Germany's his home, like it's mine. And yours. There was a huge community of them back then. Wonderful, wonderful people. So brilliant. So why shouldn't he come back here?

Ever since I turned 13, I have shot up several centimeters and can now look him straight in the eyes. They are light gray like those rocks on top of the Alps that have been exposed to the elements for thousands of years.

What really happened with the Jews? I ask.

He's not able to face me. I don't know.

But I don't drop the subject, just stand there facing him, arms folded. I notice I'm holding my breath.

It was like this, Vati says, looking over my shoulder. Once I wanted to see what all that big to-do was all about. You know. So I went to a Nazi rally. It was held inside that beautiful auditorium. I don't know if you remember it. Of course, it was bombed out in 1944, but it was the one built in the early style of—

I cut him off. And? My voice is hard. So what? I don't care about the auditorium.

EMBRYO BROTHER

A party boss was speaking. What a clown, let me tell you. Short guy, beer belly, greasy lederhosen, suspenders, knee-socks, tassels. The works. Whenever he finished a sentence, everybody jumped up. Everybody. They raised their arms in a Nazi salute and screamed Heil Hitler. That infernal noise and all those idiots. He's looking at me now. *Ach Gott*, it was disgusting.

What did you do?

I didn't jump up or salute. That's for sure. What do you think I am? A pause. So these young thugs start beating me over the head every time I don't jump up. They rolled up a stack of programs and let me have it. Whack-whack. On top of my head every time. Believe me, I got out of there just as fast as I could.

I let my breath out. That's it, that's what I've been waiting for all my life. For as long as I can remember— answers. The truth. Another deep breath: And then?

Then nothing.

My heart plummets. That's it?...You once walked out of some damn Nazi rally?

No, of course not. There was a wonderful Jewish-owned store in town. The man who came to see us worked there....Anyway, the owner and I were the best of friends. Like brothers, really. We could talk about everything. Philosophy, politics, religion. So of course I kept going there. And to pick up a few items, play some chess. You know, it was a regular corner store where you drop in. Stay as long as you like. One day I open the newspaper and see pictures of some of the people who went there with the caption:

Enemies of the People. *Mensch*, did I get furious. Enraged—that's how I felt. Violated. Those Nazi assholes, how dare they!

And then what? I say feeling better again.

Then nothing. I stopped going there. What good would it have done having my picture in the paper? Hmm? His hand lands on my shoulder. He's shaking me, trying to make me understand. Don't forget, I had a wife and kids to think about. Naturally first I checked on those poor people already branded Enemy of the People. Know what happened to them?

No.

They were hauled off in the middle of the night and never heard from again.

I shrug his hand off. Then what did you do? I notice I'm holding my breath again.

A sigh. You know, I was busy with my life's work. Anyway, I was always apolitical.

Is that the same as amoral?…

He looks at me, then: What's this? He steps closer, and I feel his hand land on my cheek, hard. He's slapped me.

Why? What? I'm reeling from the pain.

You cut your bangs, damn you.

Stunned I run my hand up to my hair line and groan inwardly. Oh no. I've forgotten to pull my hair down and hide my bangs. I was so eager to finally find out something about the Jews that I didn't make the switch from the way I look at school to home. On the way there, I always pull up my skirt, cinch my belt, pinch my cheeks to make them look red, ask one of my friends to let me borrow her cherry-red lipstick. Hope he doesn't come at me with a white hand-kerchief next. I'm sorry, I say, but that doesn't help.

Vati is raving: How dare you cut your hair? How many times have I told you not to? Next thing you'll be wearing lipstick and nail polish. All that American shit. We Germans want our girls to be natural, natur-al. Don't you understand? Don't you be going around imitating the style of loose women. All that Ami trash. What do you think this is? Think of all the men who died trying to defend the fatherland. The Nazis were idiots, sure. But that doesn't make all their ideals wrong. Pure German womanhood is what we want. Not some hussies painting themselves and....

I slump on a chair, hold my face, make sure my lips aren't visible. I should cry and he'd stop his rant-ing, I know. But I can't cry, won't cry. I hate him. Slapping me in the face is his way to get out of answering me:

Is apolitical the same as amoral?

❦ ❦ ❦

Julie keeps visiting the brand-new banks that mushroom on every square in Munich. She buys a lot in Starnberg, a town at another Bavarian lake that looks just like Diessen. She hires a contractor and subcontractor and has her dream house built. Like *this*. It's *Wirtschaftswunder* time, isn't it? Boom time in post-war *Deutschland*.

Eins, zwei, drei.

She pays some of the big bills with the borrowed money and borrows more to make the bank pay-ments. Then more for whatever other costs she has—no matter that Vati rages every evening about all those damn bills coming in. And he doesn't even see the real bills, the big ones, for the new house. Julie hides them. All she ever trots out to him are ordinary bills, pitiful small ones: for a pair of shoes for the boys. Or for staples like the flour and noodles she's charged at the latest grocery store to open up.

The other stores have stopped letting her charge anything. Too many unpaid bills.

But in the end Vati gives up. He cannot stop Julie from forging ahead with her house plans. No one can. So Vati spends most of his time in a garage across town where he keeps working on his dream while she steps up her work on hers....

He is this close again. *This* close!

One day I come home from high school, yank my skirt down to mid-calf. Lose the tight belt, rake my hair to cover the short fashionable wisps brushing against my forehead. Furiously rub off lipstick and rouge, and am pleased I didn't forget anything when I notice a small decrepit moving van just loading up the last of our rickety furniture.

What's going on? I say, afraid we've been evicted. Or maybe Vati has finally been caught tapping into the electric power on the street lights. Or some social worker has come, taken the little boys away, and the whole house of cards has collapsed.

But no, Julie is happily directing the driver: Stuff the mattresses in this way. The chairs in that way. You can load it all up....To me: Yoo-hoo, child. We're moving to Starnberg. She's wiping her hands.

I'm startled. Where?

To my new house. Oh, oh, isn't that exciting? It's not finished yet but livable. C'mon, she drags me into the cab where I squeeze in next to the driver who mumbles something about not having been paid. Julie has pressed in beside me. The little boys are already out there, she explains. Bet you can't wait to see our new place. Let's go....

But the driver won't start the motor. First my money. You promised.

Julie's face flames. I don't have any money on me right now, she says. If you stop at that branch bank on the other side of town....

No. I got to have it now or else—

Julie starts shaking like she used to every time a storm came up. Everything in her face collapses and I can't stand seeing her suffer like that.

While my five older brothers and sisters have made their fast getaway from home, I haven't been totally blind. I hoped that sooner or later I'd do the same. Graduation is only a week off. I've already found a landlady who will let me rent a room from her dirt cheap. Just a small deposit needed; she'll hold that room for me. Then my plan is to work at even more odd jobs. I can always find plenty. People just take a look at me and always immediately hire me for their worst chores, their hardest work for the cheapest wages. I'm a born slave; so be it. I'll save my money slowly and surely. Go to college eventually. Might take me a few years but that's exactly what I'm going to do.

Julie has started sobbing, I'm *this* close, *ach Gott!* *This* close. The driver says nothing, gets out and starts unloading all our junk again. Tosses our junk on the street. I can't stand Julie's crying. Here, I say and hand her all I've saved towards going to school.

Immediately Julie brightens, stands tall, chin up. Oh, yoo-hoo, driver. She gives him what she owes, plus a handsome tip. Pockets the rest and we're on our way.

I shrink into myself as the moving van trundles south. I see the green trees against the blue sky. The picturesque Munich outskirts. Sunny chapels, from which joyful church songs climb toward heaven like birds. Oh, how I wish I were anywhere but here, trapped between the driver who's grumbling because he lost time, and Julie, who's beaming. She got her way, always does.

Maybe it's for the best, I think. How much arguing can Vati and Julie do when they're separated by 30 or 40 kilometers? This move will avert a tragedy.

We lumber into Starnberg and arrive at a building site. Julie sure wasn't exaggerating when she said the house wasn't finished. We are stopped in front of a mud field that surrounds a ranch-style house that's barely been erected. The walls aren't finished but stretch and stretch. I'm amazed at how large the structure is. Is this a duplex or triplex?

The man balances on planks thrown across the brown mud and unloads rickety bedsteads, stained pillows. Dented aluminum pots, boxes of sheets that need mending. Before he rattles off, Julie gives him another generous tip. He heads for the *Gasthaus* at the corner, and she shows me around her big house. I count the many small bedrooms. There's 10 or more.

Are you going to open an inn?

No, that's all for you kids. Each of you will finally get their own room.

But everybody's gone, I say.

Uh-uh. Just look. She points out the window down to a huge puddle where my little brothers are having a mud wrestling contest.

It's going to be so hard to get those gray stains out. But that's only five, I say.

Oh, no, no. *Nein, nein.* The older ones all will come back, just you wait. And there's you *natuerlich*! Your new job starts first thing in the morning.

I have school, Mama.

Forget school. You've had your nose in too many books already. And look where it's gotten you. Nowhere, right? So I got you a good job down at the five and dime. Nice place. Fifty hours a week plus overtime....

Please, please let me finish high school first. Please. I need the diploma to get into college this fall.

Get into college? Are you crazy? You aren't going to college. You've got all the education you'll ever need, understand? Besides, who do you think's going to pay the bills around here?

I have no answer. Shrug.

You, that's who. Oh, do I need lots of new things for the house. Can't begin to name everything. *Komm, komm.* Let me show you. We've got to have rugs in the living room and hallway. Curtains in the bedrooms. And curtain rods and towels. New dishes and silverware and...and....She rambles on excitedly, and I feel trapped.

Mama, Mama! I try to stem her flow of words. We don't need all that stuff, really, and sure I'll work hard. Maybe take two jobs. Three. I can earn quite a bit, you know. But first please let me finish high school, all right? And at the end of the summer, the university part time and—?

Are you out of your mind? Your job starts at 7 AM sharp in the morning. There are shelves to stock, floors to sweep. Now c'mon, hurry, *schnell*. I've got nothing to eat in the house. And beds have to be made. Start right here. She directs me to the first bedroom. Use the best linen we got. It'll have to do until I can buy new sheets, as soon as you get your paycheck, all right? But be sure to make up this bed extra pretty, would you?

I sigh. Why? Who gets this bedroom?

Your newest little brother.

My newest brother?

Jajaja, look. Just look what that bastard of your father did to me. Got me pregnant again, son of a bitch. But I showed him. Went straight in for a hysterectomy. Didn't tell them I was pregnant. Just said that I had these terrible periods. So they cleaned me out, totally. You know, womb, everything. *Raus*. But when the nurse turned her back, I made my move. Look here. Julie unfolds a small package of wax paper she's had tucked in her pocket all along and shows me a little dead frog, about three inches long

What's that? I hold the frog up by one leg. Something the boys found in the mud?

No, that's your newest brother. Now like I told you, fix his room extra nice—

I step back, feeling like a cornered deer. Mama, Mama, Mama.

Here. She pushes the frog at me. You keep it.

No. I put my hands up, trying to distance myself from her. From the dried fetus. As soon as I can, I head for the door.

Where in the world are you going? Julie bars my way, arms folded.

I can hardly get my breath. If I'm going to quit school, don't I have to return my textbooks first?

I guess so. See if you can't catch a ride back to Munich with that driver, she says.

☙ ☙ ☙

Back in town I head for the friendly landlady and plead my case: Something's come up. Can I rent the room we talked about now? Today? Please? I don't have any other place to stay.

Sure, come on in. She asks for the deposit. Eagerly I reach in my pocket and find nothing but a few coins. My face feels flushed. I realize I have no money. I gave all I had to Julie.

Uh-oh, sorry. I think I lost it.

Then I'll just hold your room till you find it again. The landlady smiles, lets me out and embarrassed I run down the street. Follow Balanstrasse to Rosenheimer Platz and keep going. Keep striding out, deep in thought.

When I get to Marienplatz, I slow down. The coins are hot in my pocket. I know it's enough to take a bus back to Starnberg, but that's all. So good-bye, dream.

This is it. I'll be Julie's worker, her slave, for the rest of my life.

I drag myself across the magnificent square where the historical Rathaus presides in old silver-colored pomp. The architectural details are breathtaking. The Glockenspiel, silent at this time of day, draws tourists from all over. I hear them chatter around me, those throngs of visitors from all over the world. Everyone comes here for a look at the *new* Germany, the *wunder*land, and a taste of the culture and the *Bier*, some serious shopping. Sightseeing. Munich is over 1,000 years old, took major hits during the war but look! Now it's all back to pre-war splendor. Magnificent.

I slow my pace: What's the hurry? Buses run late into the night, don't they? So I can always catch another one. Seeing all the hustle and excitement, I feel old, burdened. Like my life's over already. I wanted to escape my mixed-up family, get an education, contribute to making the world better some day. Not work hard forever until I die just to put food on the table for my family and to slowly pay off all of Julie's monstrous bills.

I trudge on, feeling tears collect in the corners of my eyes. My stomach is rumbling. I haven't eaten anything all day except for a slice of *Schwarzbrot* that morning. But all around me delicious smells waft from Viktualien Markt close by, where oranges, bananas, strawberries and grapes, and carrots, kohlrabi, tomatoes and cucumbers are piled high on outdoor stands. Where chattering crowds shop. Where all kinds of delicious *Bratwurst, Knackwurst,*

Weisswurst, and *Bockwurst* are on sale. And semmels. And *Leberkaese mit Kartoffelsalat.*

Up closer new buildings sparkle. Immense window panes reflect the afternoon sun. And well-fed burghers and their beaming wives emerge from fancy restaurants and cafes. The oompah-pah Bavarian band sounds trail them like wedding gown trains.

The happy new Germans burp with satisfaction after their delicious lunches of *Schweinsbraten und Knoedel.* Or their desserts of *Kirsch Kuchen mit Schlag.* All of Bavaria has risen from the ashes, dusted itself off. Is wearing brand-new outfits, coats of paint. Prosperity abounds everywhere I look. There's a feeling of success permeating the air. The toot-tooting horns of the BMWs, the black Mercedes taxis with their big-bellied drivers in uniforms are all fitting props in this spectacle of *nouveaux riches*-ness.

Such life; such abundance. Newspaper boys hawk packets of crisp papers: Sueddeutsche Zeitung! Street vendors boast of their wares: luscious blueberries, golden apples, graceful stalks of fresh white asparagus piled on carts. The cherries are giant rubies, turning sidewalks into jewelry exhibits.

The air is clean. The sky, limitless. Everyone's surging toward exciting days and nights ahead. Carry with them their latest purchases from stores bulging with imported leather goods from Florence, Italy. Gold chains from Barcelona, Spain. Dresses in emerald silk, satin and brocade from Paris swath mannequins that preen in elaborate window displays. They look real. And girls and boys my age saunter past, arms linked, their eyes shining, their steps lively.

They all look well fed, well dressed, well liked. Cared for.

Someone gives a damn about them.

I rub my hands, trying to forget the feel of the frog.

I walk so slowly that people have to push me aside to get past. I know exactly what my future will be like. I know how my life will play out: Tomorrow I'll start toiling at the job Julie has picked out for me, and that's it: There's a life sentence waiting for me.

And it's not just the physical labor that will wear me down. It's those unanswered questions that I have, even now. Stop, I want scream at the celebrating masses. Stop. Scratch the surface. Look beneath. Think!

Remember! Think back!

How can you forget so soon?...

The light suffusing Marienplatz changes. It's getting dark. Time to go. To head out to Starnberg. Begin serving my life sentence....

As I drag myself away from Marienplatz, I see out of the corner of my eye a most unusual man crossing the square from the opposite direction. A shock of totally white hair surrounds his handsome well-boned face. Under straight brows his light gray eyes look off into the distance. He walks with a surprisingly athletic gait for someone his age and the way he cuts through the crowd shows he's a leader. Someone extraordinary. Suddenly he focuses on the crowd, sees me and heads my way.

What're you doing here, Eri? Vati says, using his nickname for me. He knows who I am.

I bring my hand up to my hair in a rush, but cannot feel any short strands poking out. I'm on my way back out to Starnberg, I say. We moved into the new house today,

I heard about it. So why so glum?

Because I don't want to move out there. I really don't.

Why?

I want to stay here in Munich, finish school.

Can't you go to school out there?

No, she won't let me. She says I've got too much education already.

Well, maybe she's right. Education's never done me any good. So go on, try your best, work hard and—

But I really don't want to. Julie is…I don't know how to explain the fetus in wax paper. She's not well.

Ach ja, ja, ja. I'm not either.

I'm sorry. I don't disagree with him.

Never mind, Eri, he says. What good are regrets? He gives a dismissive wave. What good is wishing for what wasn't meant to be?…So what would you like to do?

Stay here in Munich, Vati. Graduate, then get a job, or lots of different jobs. And save some money so I can go to the University.

A flicker in his eyes. What for?

I don't know, but someday I want to go somewhere, do something. Make a difference.

What do you mean?

I want to make things better.

Why? It's all better now, don't you see? No more Nazis. Just look around. The ruins are all gone. No signs left of the war. Don't you know it's a fantastic miracle, this new land of ours in the era of the *Wirtschaftswunder*? Aren't you proud?

No. I can't forget what it's built on. Oh, Vati. The blood of all those innocent people is in this soil. When I look at this new prosperity, all I think is Dachau. Dachau. I can't forget it—and I don't see how you can.

He looks ashamed. I never really thought—Well, I was always just so wrapped up in my new inventions.

Dammit. Are inventions more important than human beings?

He looks pained, has no answer.

I go on: I guess it's no use to dream. It was just a dumb idea anyway. I've always been the *Dummkopf* of the family. The *flasche*, the wimp. I've done nothing but ask stupid questions all my life and I'm still looking for answers....Fact is I can't afford to stay in this town. So I'd better catch the next bus out to Starnberg now...*Wiedersehn*...I turn to leave, walk away.

Wait. Vati pulls out his flat old wallet. There's nothing in there, I know. He's broke, he always is. But from deep inside, from a hidden compartment he extracts some crisp notes—his emergency *gelt*. Every last bit of it. It's the money he's been saving for years and years in case there's ever a WW III. It's all the money he has, all he will ever have.

Here. Take this.

I feel tears streaming down my face. Vati, oh Vati, no. I can't take this.

You must. His voice and look are stern. People stop and stare at us. He waves them on, and they obey like we kids used to when we were little.

Turning his attention back to me, he goes on: Escape, you hear me? Don't go back out to Starnberg. Just call Julie, tell her you're not coming.

I find myself trembling. But she's going to cry so hard. She's going to beg me, plead with me, I don't think I can do it—

Then I'll call her, he cuts me off, giving me a nudge. Now go, go. Go! Go away and live.

Tears streaming down my face, I hug him. Stumble off, the *gelt* hot in my hand. It's enough to let me make a deposit on the room and stay in Munich. That allows me to finish the Gymnasium. And I continue to pick up all the odd jobs I can get until I can afford to move closer to Schwabing, the university section of Munich, where I learn to walk with my head high.

❦ ❦ ❦

There, a year later, I'm sitting at a big round wooden table with a dozen young men, all students, one late afternoon. I'm catching my breath between jobs; they, between lectures and labs. There are co-eds too, but having grown up with so many brothers, I get along better with males. One of them, Philip, who likes me and has an artist's eye, says to me: I have a friend I want you to meet.

Why?

Because you two would look good together. You're both tall, slim, dark-haired....And fascinating.

Well, why not? I say with a shrug, not knowing that my life is about to change.

The friend turns out to be a young, narrow-shouldered man over six foot, with thick black curly hair, green eyes and freckles. An American soldier from Rocky Mount, North Carolina. He interrupted his college education in the U.S. to enlist in the army. Yet he doesn't carry any arms. He's an orderly with the Second Field Hospital in Munich. That means, his work is healing.

Not hurting.

After Philip makes the introduction the next day, he fades forever from my field of vision. I'm that taken with the soldier, who wears dungarees with a razor crease and a button-down snowy shirt, sleeves rolled up to reveal well-muscled forearms and beautiful hands.

He looks like a boy barely into his teens, with a narrow waist, a carefree walk and energy to spare. And his smile is as blinding as his white shirt; all his teeth are lined up in perfect formation.

What's more amazing: He's a bookworm too. Loves to read just like me. Except he's starting from scratch with the reading, the studying, the thinking. He comes from a family of farmers; his grandfather only went to the second grade. His father to the eleventh.

My soldier is the first in his immediate family ever to attend college.

No wonder he can walk with such a free stride. Can step boldly forward. He doesn't have any of the accumulated weight of family intellect, compounding over the centuries until it crowded out compassion, burdening him down.

Oh no, he's his own boy-man.

Quickly we discover more common ground: He

likes to ponder problems just for the heck of them. I ponder them for survival. But the process is the same—think hard about something, real hard, then speculate out loud about it if there's someone willing to listen.

I am that someone.

I listen with every fiber, not only for the underlying meaning of what he says, but also because of the sheer novelty of the language, on which I'm trying to get a grip.

And I enjoy listening to his soothing Southern voice whose sound is the antithesis of the cold consonant-crammed German tongue, that terrible tongue uttered by the concentration camp commandos when they made their *selections*. That horrible barking, bolstered by the flashing of firearms:

Schnell! Schnell! Step lively now.

You! This way, off to hard labor....

You! That way, off to the ovens....

My soldier talks softly without weapons. He's trained to tend to wounds, bring balm. Ease pain.

On his days off from the army, he enjoys strolling to the Viktualien market and picking up some semmels, salami, sliced Edam and a couple bottles of Lowenbrau. Packs a pastel hospital blanket, goes to the English Gardens, selects a sunny spot by the babbling Isar River, spreads out the blanket just so. Sits down. Eats, reads a paragraph of Plato and ponders out loud about what's wrong with the world....

Whenever I have a half hour free, I join him on the warm blanket. I make sure I sit as far away from the

Isar as I can, though. Don't want to be anywhere near the spot where *Reichsmarshall* Hermann Goering's ashes might have been dumped after his corpse was burned in the Dachau crematorium in 1946. Everyone knows that his remains were pitched into a Munich brook....

The thought should ruin my appetite, but I can't help myself. Always ravenous, I dive into the delectable picnic foods spreading out like a fan. I stuff myself. Listen to the ideas of my peaceful soldier and am in awe of his life of ease. What Eden. All he does is work 40 to 50 hours a week; the rest of the time his life is his own, mostly.

It's heady to know someone who has such power over his own existence. I have hardly any over mine.

Soon my soldier devotes all his free time to me. We have so much to talk about, especially once we decide to split up our areas of interest. I get to ruminate over the things of the past, while he concentrates on the now and the future. So seamlessly we're covering the development of mankind, starting with Adam and Eve.

Soon everybody accepts us as the "serious" couple.

But all our time isn't devoted to just deep thought. We have moments of sheer radiance too, when there's nothing but the vast green expanse of the beautiful park under us and the Bavarian sky a blue glass bowl above. For a few miraculous minutes I shed my persona of a middle-aged, overworked post-WW II woman, old long before her time.

Now I'm a young girl, spending time with a boy-man who can be so funny.

EMBRYO BROTHER

On our second date, he jokes about marrying me.
Turns out he's not joking.

CHAPTER 16

Ur-Cry

An ordinary day for me, but a good one: My soldier is off on an "alert" in Northern Germany. That's a military game lasting for weeks which rehearses the GIs in case WW III should ever break out. They leave Munich for days, head to unpopulated areas, where they sleep in comfortable tents, get plenty of rations, chase each other through the woods, and patch up pretend-war victims. What fun.

Yet for once I'm having fun too, bustling around in a neat small shop tucked into a fashionable Munich side street and am humming. There are many such establishments. When the city was rebuilt, the first floors of the huge apartment buildings downtown were usurped by merchants. Window-shopping is the dream leisure activity of the *new* Germans now, second only to real shopping. After years of being surrounded by drab ruins, people hunger for color and opulence. Luxury. And that's available again, in fancy fashion displays, in the luscious fresh produce available everywhere, in the butcher shops where slab after slab of red juicy meat vies for attention.

I can't afford to buy anything, but I can feast my eyes on the abundance, can't I?

How much change has occurred in the last few years: No more ration cards, no more black market, no more national starvation. Money is flowing again everywhere like the strong currents in the Isar River after a rainstorm. Life is a rosy dawn in the big population centers and the small towns and villages.

For me too. I never have trouble getting hired and enjoy the simple jobs I'm asked to do in whatever temporary position I'm occupying at the moment. There's an office in Schwabing where college students and those on the verge of becoming college students sign up and pay a small fee.

For that they're entered in an odd-jobs registry. And every week they can pick up all kinds of temporary work assignments. And those jobs pay real cash. Wow. The pinched woman behind a small glass window doles out little pastel paper slips with the names of the firms, the addresses, and the hourly wages. I grab as many as I'm allowed to and hop to it. Work a few hours in one store, a few more in another. Add to that by part-time baby-sitting for a family with four boys. Make a few extra *Deutsche Marks* by doing some window washing for a professor....

And so on.

Often I work 16 hours a day, which is nothing.

Back when I was still at home, I kept going 20 hours a day, with nothing to show for it. Now finally I see my savings grow. And another great thing: All that nonstop working exhausts me so that I don't have to think. So as long as I'm on the go, I really don't think of Germany's crimes against humanity or of home.

But when I slow down I still do. I ask myself for the zillionth time: How can a country that's so bright and beautiful have been so brutal?

And I think of Julie in her half-finished house in Starnberg. And the poor little boys. Who's going to look after them now when Julie has another nervous breakdown? Who's feeding them supper? Helping them with their spelling and reading? Getting their school clothes ready?

Scrubbing their grimy little necks?

Does she really put that *thing*, that frog, to bed every night?

I shudder at the thought, at how bad off Julie might be soon. No, no, I realize. It's now. She was in the midst of a breakdown when I last saw her, when I left and never came back. I walked out on a very sick woman and feel rotten about it.

But aren't those boys *her* kids? Ever since I can remember I've been helping her raise them. I've been keeping them for her. I've been helping Julie.

When is my time?

Now.

I make a tight fist, punch the air. Punch it hard. *Ja, ja. Ja.* Won't be much longer now before I can become a full-time student. I've already signed up for the first semester, but the price of the university fees and the textbooks keeps going up. Up. Everything's getting so expensive in Munich.

So: Could I please have a few more work assignment slips? I beg the dispenser of odd jobs at the small student-aid office at the University of Munich. She's noticed I always grab a fistful. Thin-lipped, she doles out a few more little slips and reminds me that once I take them, I'm obliged to do the work. No excuses.

I nod eagerly. There isn't a job in the world I can't do faster and better than anyone else. Of course, I'm hoping none of the assignment slips will dispatch me right back to that hellish brush factory. Fortunately, none ever does. But there are some jobs that are just about as awful. One is a wrapping assignment.

I report to a grim building off Sendlinger Tor Platz where I have to check hubcaps that tumble off an assembly line. I must find any and all flaws, set the rejects aside, wrap the good ones individually in butcher paper squares. Quick, quick, *mach schnell*. Center all perfect hubcaps on the paper, fold the four corners just so. Stack the big wrapped disks into towers of many dozens, pack them in boxes. *Schneller!*

OK. I got it, nothing to it. Roll up my sleeves. Massage my old, calloused hands.

But the hubcaps are sharp-edged and vicious. They bite my skin. The harsh paper cuts my flesh deeper, and the fine metal shavings, which waft like clouds of dust motes in the giant room where I hunch at a table with other day laborers, settle into the open wounds and fester there.

But no time to try to dig them out until the evening when my shift is over.

By then my hands are swollen and stiff. I can picture the metal filings entering my bloodstream and traveling around in my body. Won't they be surprised when they come up against my glue-filled lungs? No passage here. Ha. I soak my aching hands, clean out the numerous cuts. Swab them with iodine.

Smarts like *Hoelle*. The fierce burning brings tears to my eyes, but hey! I'm making good money, right? And every weekend my hands have a chance to heal. At least I don't have to look at them much. Heda lets me have an old pair of gloves.

Worse is my next job—proofreading what looks like military dog tags. I report to another sinister-looking building in downtown Munich. This time I have to perch on a three-legged stool between two moving bands. On my right small metal tags shoot down a moving band past me. They sport long numbers, nonsensical letters and dots stamped on them, which I scan with one eye. While with the other I read lists of information printed on long wide strips of paper that rush past me on the left. This job is to catch any discrepancies between the data on paper and that encoded and stamped on the metal tags. When I find something wrong, I'm to snatch the offending dogtag off the moving band. Send it packing back to the head of the line for re-stamping.

No metal shavings here, thank heavens. So no cuts on my hands and no devilish, harsh wrapping paper that can slice my palms to ribbons. No metal filings clogging up my innards either.

Gut!

But the constant focus on all those numbers, letters and dots gives me a headache and after less than an hour I feel as if I'd been axed in half. Vertically. The problem is that my eyes have different jobs to do. Reading figures on paper is easy; on metal tags, it's hard. So my left eye has the easy job, while my right one must strain constantly.

And coordinating all this incoming information and concentrating nonstop so I'll automatically toss out the misprinted tags is pure murder. Often I snatch at the paper rather than the incorrect dog tag. Or there's a slight delay in my mind's processing. It's only after the incorrectly stamped tag has passed by me that I know with certainty it has an error. So I have to stop the band, track the faulty tag down, while more work is piling up for me, which makes me have to speed up later on.

But worse is overlooking a mistake that is invariably caught by a checker in another room who always screams in outrage.

It's driving me crazy, the unceasing pressure not to overlook a single misplaced numeral or letter or dot. Sometimes it's only the sequence of the characters that's wrong or the spacing. Instead of seventeen tiny dots, there may be eighteen. Or sixteen. Oh, everything begins to blur after a while.

I get jumpy. Wince a lot. I'm always afraid to hear the screams. Long series of numbers and letters dance in front of my eyes all the time. After work I can hardly see anything. My eyes feel they've done enough for one day and quit cold.

Or they strike out individually. One eye sees something on the right while the other travels off to the left. I bump into people on my way home. I over-look breaks in the pavement, start to stumble on per-fectly even ground. Even after I finally sit still on some bench in the *Englische Garten*, figures swirl in my head and I jerk, as if someone has slapped me.

Each day I have to go against what comes natur-al—my two eyes working in concert. At night I wake up with a sharp pain behind the eyes. I have trouble reading anything without focusing on the shapes of letters, the arrangements of numbers, dots, dots, dots. But the money is *verdammt* good.

So is the pay for washing dishes in the *Bayerische Hof,* one of the finest hotels and restaurants in Munich.

No sharp objects here. No letters, numbers. Ahh. All the beautiful, ornamental silver forks, spoons and knives go right into the giant dishwashers. I'd like to steal a few, pawn them, but an assistant cook says: That asshole head housekeeper counts them each day.

Oh well.

At least there's no complicated watching-out for dumb dots involved. My eyes can go on vacation here. All I have to do is make sure every dish is sparkling by the end of my work time. I smile, for this job is a perfect match for me. Julie would be so pleased if she could see me.

I load and unload the many dishwashers. First I help myself to what's left on the plates, yum! Scrape what I can't eat onto a napkin to take home later. Never had it better. Until I get to the dozens of enor-mous black pots and pans.

They don't fit in the dishwasher and are caked on. Have to be scrubbed good. But to get down in them I have to climb into the giant sink. Fancy food particles spray in all directions as I scrub away. Still some pots won't cooperate. Their gunk is ingrained. So I scrape and peck and chip away at the bottoms of the giant pots. Attack the dried food remnants, using spatulas, ladles, and scrapers like pickaxes. Employ whatever sharp and pointy metal tools I can get my hands on.

Greasy water splashes on the kitchen floor. I'm up to my ankles in it. Slosh around wearily. My back aches. My shoulders scream. My arms tremble: one monster pot done, three dozen to go.

I work all evening and night. The vast kitchen quiets down. Only a skeleton staff left, counting dishes, smoking, drinking schnapps.

By four in the morning I'm down to my last dozen pots, have food particles all over my clothes. Tomato freckles on my face. I walk like an old woman, finally finish the last pot at 7 AM, get my pay, 10 marks.

Ah, cool cash. Another step closer to becoming a genuine college kid. I caress the bill. Sure earned every pfennig of it and many times over.

I stumble out into the cool morning. Another brilliant Munich day has begun with a dark-blue limitless sky. Peaked clouds like whipped cream hang from it. Far in the distance I see the majestic Alps. Such beauty everywhere. Such hope. But I can barely put one foot in front of the other. The soles of my feet feel scalded. There's no way that I can walk to where I live, three kilometers away. I'll be lucky if I can make it to the end of the block.

A taxi rescues me, delivers me to my student quarters, where I rouse. The driver says, eight marks. I give it to him, plus a good tip, which wipes out the 10 marks I earned.

I crawl inside the building to my room, fall into bed. I've got two whole hours before my next job starts.

This is an easy one, in one of those little quaint stores on a side street.

❦ ❦ ❦

A plum assignment. I get to sit down comfortably part of the time. Get to take a break between the easy work which consists of unpacking small items, knick-knacks, gifts. Shelving them and keeping track of them. Answering the phone, which rings often: Rrring-ring. It means I'll be writing down orders. I enjoy that, taking those phone orders. For here nothing is dangerous, damaging, detrimental to my health. Nothing exhausts me totally. Nothing and no one is driving me crazy. I don't have to constantly fear that I'll collapse, die prematurely from overwork.

What a relief. This is just a nice part-time job on a quiet Munich street, which will not totally drain me. In the evening I will have some energy left, for once in my life. So I think ahead excitedly: Should I go to Schwabing after I finish work today? Buy some of my textbooks in advance...? Ride the streetcar, instead of all that walking I usually do?

Go eat in a restaurant?

I swallow. Yes! I've never done that before: go in the front door of a restaurant, sit down at a table, get a menu, order something, eat it, and pay for it. This time I won't enter from the back, head straight for the kitchen, tackle the dishes while munching on whatever's left over on the plates of strangers.

For a moment I massage my poor hands. Slip out of my ugly shoes and rub my worn-out feet. They've done so much work, so much walking already. I'm not yet 20, and my hands and feet look like I'm 90.

But it doesn't have to be that way anymore. Now I have choices. Should I splurge and buy some Nivea lotion? Smear the lotion on my hands and feet? Get some nail polish too while I'm at it? Vati has no hold over me anymore. He set me free. Told me to live. Live. I can be my own person now, responsible only for myself. I'm so excited realizing that I can finally splurge a little. Maybe even take a day off one day soon....

Have some time to be!

Of course, I'm humming now. Who wouldn't hum? I stand up, stretch. My life's working out great. Finally. To get paid for doing this easy work is incredible. And I almost have all the money I need for a whole year of studying. I'm at paradise's door, already looking in.

The phone again. Rrring-ring. Heda. Something in her voice makes me feel like a bucket of ice dunked over me.

What's the matter?

Vati came to see me early this morning, she says. He looked awful.

Why, what's happened?

Julie died.

I sit down. Oh no. That's terrible. What happened?

I don't know.

What do you mean, you don't know. Didn't Vati tell you?

No, he just dropped Karli off and that—Karli is the youngest brother, only five years old. The others are now old enough to look after themselves for a few days. Heda is still talking—was all. Vati asked me to keep him. Can you come and get him? I'm busy.

Heda is married now with her own kids. She didn't manage to snare an aristocrat. Instead, it's someone from East Germany, a hard-working young man. An *only* child! Amazing. But her climb back up in society demands that she ride horses, attend women's lunches, have her teeth capped, facials every week.... Of course, she can't look after Karli. And Ger is still in Augsburg, where she continues to get accolades for her artistic talents.

And naturally, the older boys are all already enmeshed in all kinds of work that has a future. Or they have left the country. I'm the only one in limbo, have a handful of odd jobs to see to, but there's nothing permanent. I'm not yet officially in college, so it's me again that's stuck.

Yes, I say, sighing. I can take Karli. Just let me finish this job—

Hurry. Heda.

I will...so tell me. What happened?

Heda sounds cross and wants to get off the phone fast. I told you I don't know.

But I can't believe it and push on: Come on. Julie just died like that? What illness did she have?

None that I know of.

Then what was it? What? An accident?

Must have been. I hear Heda's low moan. She goes on: Vati just said she fell over dead. He went out to Starnberg to see her last night. She's been trying to get him to come out and see the new house. And when he got there, they had a few words.

A few words? I find myself pacing in place. What does that mean?

Draw your own conclusion, Eri.

A fight, then. OK. A big one. How terrible was it?

Jesus. I don't know. He said he didn't touch her. But suddenly he said it all came crashing down on him....

What? The unfinished house?

No, Dummkopf. All of it, the damn war, his missed opportunities. Germany. His women, his whole damn fucked-up life!

Heda!

Don't Heda me, Eri. I'm sick of this shit. What do you know about anything?

I suck in air. Gulp. Nothing, I answer. That's why I'm asking you what happened. I want to know. Tell me. How can Julie just die? I saw her not long ago and she was all right, physically that is. You know what I mean. So what the hell happened to her? I'm rocking on my heels, shove the little trinkets aside with my free hand. Or do I have to come out to your house right now and drag it out of you?

No, don't come. Don't you dare come out here. I have enough on my shoulders already. Don't you know how hard it's been on me? Trying to separate myself from—? And here Vati comes and drops that snot-nosed little kid on my doorsteps. Christ.

I said I'd take him. Dammit, Heda. I try to calm her down. So...so? I go on impatiently. Tell me everything. Vati says he snapped. Big deal. What I want to know is, how did Julie die? Did he hurt her?

That's what I asked too, Eri. But he denied it, said she just fell down dead.

That doesn't make any sense, Heda.

Well....She's searching for an explanation: Maybe in his crazy condition...? Maybe he didn't know what happened. Might be he blacked out and when he came to, that's what he saw.

So then what happened? Did he call a doctor? The ambulance?

He took her to the emergency room.

What did they say?

That she was dead.

Jesus Christ, I explode. That poor man. Must really be totally nuts....I shake my head. Always knew it would come to a bad end.

Same here, says Heda. That's why I was so desperately trying to get out of the house. Distance myself from all of you. And now look. More than likely there'll be something about it in the paper. I'll be mentioned as one of the survivors. Damn, damn, damn. What will people think? It's so embarrassing. Plus, them not living together.

And all those bills, I throw in.

Shit. I forgot about that. Who's going to pay for her funeral? Vati has nothing.

I know, I know. *Not long ago he gave me his last gelt.* My thoughts are wild birds trapped in a cage. Heda, I have a little money saved up—

Good, good, then that's settled.

But not enough for the bills—

How much do you think they add up to?

With that new house? It's bound to be in the thousands. And not a penny's been paid. Didn't you know?

No. I have my own problems. The equestrian society fees are due, you can't ride in the English Gardens without the proper getup. The planning committee for the Opera season meets tomorrow. And the registration is due for our annual ski trip to Kitzbuehel. The maid wants a raise. We need a new car. You've got no idea what it costs living like we do, keeping up with the—

I cut Heda off: Oh no! What about all those banks? Once they read about Julie's death they will all come calling immediately with their hands out....But maybe Vati can ask for an extension on those loans? Surely as sick as he is, they have to take that into consideration—?

One thing at a time, Heda says, all right? Now when can we meet and where? So I can transfer Karli to you?

By then I have calmed down. I know that I can afford to stop working for a little while, look after Karli, cook some food and take it out to Starnberg for the older boys, so they won't go hungry. I can look after Vati too, make sure he gets something to eat, help him with the funeral arrangements....Let's meet this afternoon at Rosenheimer Platz.

Why not now? Or at lunch?

Because first I have to find Vati, get him squared away. Where is he?

I don't know.

Did he go back to the hospital?

I don't know.

Dammit, Heda. You're the smartest of 11 kids. Where did he say he was going?

To the police.

Why? You said he didn't hurt Julie.

Right, but according to him, the hospital said they'd give him only a couple of hours.

For what?

To get his affairs in order.

Meaning what?

To get the boys taken care of, I guess. Find a babysitter for Karli.

But why? Why?

Because they plan to turn him in.

To a mental institution?

No. To the police.

Are they crazy? He didn't hurt Julie. You just told me that's what he said.

Right, right. Heda sounds frustrated. That's exactly what he said.

So she just up and died. That's nothing to get the police involved in. People die every day. Maybe Julie had a heart attack.

Sure, that's what I think too, Eri. It was some sort of heart attack. Except—

Except what?

That time problem. You see, Vati took Julie to the hospital first thing this morning, right before he brought Karli here—

And?

She died last night.

When?

About nine or 10 o'clock.

What in the world? What was he thinking? Didn't he know she was dead? What made him wait so long, for heaven's sake? Questions keep flooding my mind, are out of my mouth.

I asked him the very same thing. That's when he told me it all came crashing down on him, whatever that means, and I guess he lost his head. First he tried to revive her frantically, tried everything he could. Oh, he sounded so frightened when he told me that, so pitiful. Eri, you've got to get to the bottom of it.

I will. A pause then I ask her: You mean he spent all night trying to make Julie come back to life?

No, no, only at first. Then he really lost it.

What did he do?

He drove around.

Left Julie lying dead in the house and drove around?

No.

No, what?

He took her with him.

I have to swallow hard to keep from crying openly. My eyes blur. He took Julie, I mean her body, in the car with him and drove around?

Yes, drove around all night trying to think of what to do.

My God, Heda. What if there was a chance she was still alive?

No, no, she was dead. Good and dead.

Gott in Himmel! That lunatic! All night long he

drove around with her dead beside him? How did he get her in the car?...Where did he drive to?

Heda moans again. I don't know, but I think—I think he drove to Cologne.

That's a long distance. Whatever for?

He didn't tell me, but I think he was trying to figure out a way to get rid of her. You know, dump her body somewhere....But he couldn't so he turned around and came back.

But why would he want to get rid of her? If he didn't kill her? That doesn't make sense.

I think he felt guilty, Eri.

About the way he treated her?

Sure, that too, but mostly about the way he lived, you know. Coming from that fine Vierling family and being the most talented one...You know...?

Yeah, that damn genius!

Right, so all his life he's been so smart, gotten out of a lot of stuff he's done, sort of like, well, Germany.... He's always considered himself above the law. Anyway suddenly he finds himself in real trouble. He's totally innocent this time but has this corpse on his hands. And he just freaks out....Can't you just picture him getting panicked?

Sure I can. He's finally gotten caught, but this time for something he didn't do....But, Heda, listen. All his other stuff was just minor, so I still don't get it.

Well, there's another possibility. Maybe he was really planning to kill her but before he could, she drops dead. Think of all the guilt he's feeling. It's made him go totally off his rocker...

Hmm, you're right. Maybe that's it then. Poor

man, did talk a lot about wanting her dead.

So did she.

Right. I heard her many times.

See there? That's another possibility. She just had another one of her nervous breakdowns.

I know that's the case, sure—

But maybe this time she turned violent. Suddenly jumped on him, attacked him. Couldn't take it anymore either. Maybe all those bills she had came due at the same time and she went bonkers—

No, that doesn't seem plausible to me. Why then would she suddenly fall down dead? I can't picture that scenario at all.

Then why was Vati wearing makeup?

I feel a punch in my stomach. He was wearing makeup?

Yes, I saw it, clear as day. He had these big blobs of makeup on the chin, neck. His wrists and hands. He was covering up something.

What?

Bruises, I guess.

Then...maybe she did beat him up. I'm warming to the idea. Yes, yes. I see. Her nervous breakdown made her extra strong and he had to fight back. So it was self-defense, OK? Sure. That's it. It'll be embarrassing for him to have to admit he got beaten up by his wife. But maybe that's exactly what happened.

I wish, Heda says. For if that's the case this nightmare wouldn't last long. I mean, the coroner can tell right away what somebody dies of, right? So if it was self-defense, they'll have to let him go. No question about it. But that still doesn't explain his driving

around all night and trying to dump her body somewhere.

No, it doesn't, you're right. But you said he went
crazy. So I'm sure a psychiatrist can explain that.
Here's this handsome brilliant man who has everything. Next thing he knows he's lost everything. His
business and all his money. His sister Erna whom he
loved best dies, his brother is a prisoner of war in
Siberia. All his inventions come to nothing but shit.

Because he can't ever reinvent what he once had,
Heda says. Once he had this most ingenious idea, but
then he lost it. Poof! Never could get it back....

Richtig. And then his wife dies. *Ja, ja.* Our beautiful little Mutti. Barbara, our mama bear. I feel a tear
roll down my cheek.

Yes, Eri. And then because of that damn war, he
ends with a mental patient for his second wife. Has
11 kids. And not a pot to piss in. No food, nothing.
Everything he's ever had and done turns to pure
Scheisse.

I agree with Heda. Plus, think about his country.
What a mess that turned into. A proud man like him
must've hated Hitler, that son of a bitch, I say. Hitler
ruined Germany and you know how Vati loves the
Alps, Bavaria, nature, the great Germannia. Hitler
turned it into a cemetery.

Jajaja, everything Vati loved turned into *Scheisse.*
Poor man. Everything he wanted got so damn fucked
up. It would be bad enough if Vati were just an ordinary man. But to come from so much, ride so high
one moment, then crash so low—

Right. It's worse than being dead. Really. Don't

you think so, Heda? Wonder why he never committed suicide?

Me too. You think he will now, Eri? Try to…?

Sure hope not.…Panic grips me. Oh, let's hope not. Suddenly I feel such an urgency to find Vati, reassure him that I'll do all I can to get things straightened out. Heda, I say. As soon as I've made sure he's all right, I'll call you right away. I'll take Karli, it's the least I can do. I feel guilty because I left Julie in the condition she was in. I should have stayed in Starnberg, helped her somehow. Gone to work at that dime-store job she found for me. Been there for her.… Heda, I repeat, before hanging up. Think hard. Where could Vati be? Where might he have gone after reporting Julie's death to the police?

I haven't the slightest idea, she says sounding relieved because I'm going to take over. I'm going to straighten out this mess.

Think, I implore her. Think. Think!

Only silence from her.

Well, what's the address of his old garage?

Now Heda whooshes out air. I don't know. I've never seen it, don't care to either. You know how I've avoided contact with.…Abruptly she starts screaming: Oh, why is this happening to *me*? Why? All I ever wanted was to be the child of an ordinary couple, a stupid old fart of a father, a fat dumpling mother. Not this insanity—

I scream back at her: And all I ever wanted was to be born into a country where innocent people weren't gassed and used for firewood, OK?…A pause. Are you there, Heda?

Yes, sure. Now Heda's voice sounds wracked by crying. Oh Eri...Eri...Eri....I'm just so shocked... about the whole thing...I don't know what to do. All my life I fought to get back what the war destroyed. I don't mean just money. But the standing of the family. I wanted to make it rise again. And now this shit. I'm ruined....Totally....This will make headlines, don't you see?...Such a scandal. I'm finished....She explains: You know Vati still looks good. And Julie always had all these dumb women fawning over her. So can't you just picture the gossip rags? They'll have a field day. The radio stations too. She drops her voice: Was it murder? Or something more sinister?...She sounds more like herself again as she goes on: Vati did work on those Junker airplanes, whether he wanted to or not. He did do his part in the war. So this is how the papers will blow it up: Is this a revenge killing by unknown forces? Or was it an act of jealousy by one of Vati's other women? Or by the husband of one of those women?

She takes a deep breath and goes on: *Ach*, I can see it already. They'll take a mannequin, dress it up like Julie. Have an actor with silver hair and a heart-throb face pose as Vati. Photograph him carrying her to a car with this caption: Where did Dr. Hans Vierling carry his dead wife after he killed her? And what did he do with her for however many hours passed before he took her to the hospital?—

Stop, Heda. Stop! I can't take any more.

You? Pshaw! What have you got to worry about? Nobody knows you. But what about *me*? How can I face all my friends? My clubs? My hairdresser? What about my in-laws and their—?

Shut up. Dammit, Heda. Just shut up. I don't have time for this. I need to know where Vati is. Now. Every second he could get closer to harming himself—

Don't worry about that, Eri. Just...don't...worry ...about...that.

So you know where he is?

Yes! I called already, he's safe.

Thank God for that, Heda. Thank God. I hope they've given him some medicine.

I doubt it, but he's safe. I didn't want to tell you, but they took his belt, shoes and—

What're you talking about?

What do you think, Eri? Huh? They booked him, dammit. He's behind bars, so don't worry about him, OK? You've got other stuff to worry about. Karli, for one thing. The other boys need looking after too. I guess someone has to notify the rest of the family. I can't. But you better go right ahead. You don't want them to get the bad news from the papers. Do the most important stuff first. The other things can wait, like placing the other boys with the rest of the family, getting their clothes together, packing up everything—

Hold it. You sound like Vati's going to be gone a long time.

The policeman I talked to said to expect the investigation to take anywhere from six months to a year. They'll keep him locked up until they can sort all this out.

What?

Jaja. And Ger doesn't even know about it, or Hansi. *Ach, Gott,* and what about the older boys,

Julie's sons from her first husband? See what you can find out, Eri. Please. Maybe their addresses are in Starnberg. You'd better close down that place quick too. Unless you want to be embarrassed when they come with an eviction notice. Furthermore if I were you, I wouldn't want to be there when the people in town find out what happened. Starnberg is such a small town.

Yes, right. My face flames. I've got to get out there, hide the evidence—

What evidence?

The fetus! But I don't tell Heda about it. She's distraught enough already. Oh, nothing, nothing, I say. I've just got to make sure everything's all right. Reporters will come snooping around. And just think what this will do in Diessen....

Yes. Folks will have a real ball there. Heda pauses, I can hear her blow her nose. Once, twice. She says in a changed voice: You know, Eri, I did ask your favorite question. Once. Yes, I really did. I asked our cousins.

Those who got sent home by the black Amis?

Right, those two. And you know what? They *knew*, they *knew*. Just teenagers they were then, young kids but they knew. It was around 1943 or '44. They said Aunt Hedi took them aside one day. She was just a young girl herself. She said, Do you know what they're doing to *them*? And her face was horror-struck. So it was general knowledge even among the younger generation.

Oh, Heda. Why didn't you ever tell me?

What good would that have done, Eri? You were

three or four at the time of that conversation—

No, I mean later when I got older.

It was too late then. The Jews had been killed. Millions and millions of them.

But still I would've preferred knowing about it. Instead of always wondering about *it*. So...did Vati know?

I don't know. But I think if the rest of the family knew, how could he not have known? Not at first, I think. I think he was clueless then. But later toward the end, he had to have known—

Dammit, Heda! Why did you keep me in the dark all this time? I slam the phone down. Storm out of the quaint little store onto the street and feel nothing. My legs have no sensation below the knee. I'm walking on stumps.

I stumble through Munich, a city bursting with vitality. A new world, bright and shiny, with prosperity everywhere. Men and women parade in fashionable clothes. Expensive cars zoom past, jockey for position on the wide, flower-embroidered streets. It's 1960—15 years after WW II. And there's no sign there's ever been a war here. No sign of the six million killed. It's as if Dachau was just a brief nightmare. Now Germany's awoken from a long sleep—like Snow White. A gaggle of pretty girls my age surge around me and go on, giggling about the fortune they just spent on luscious lipstick, pink powder, sheer hosiery, new nail enamel.

Let's pick up a newspaper, one girl says, as she prances past me. I heard an interesting story on the radio this morning. You won't believe it. It was so wild. All about this prominent man. Doctor of some kind. Good-looking too, and what he did last night.... Gruesome....

I feel my ears burn. Totter into an alley on legs that are stilts. Still no feeling beneath the knees. The blood must've all rushed to my heart to deal with the shock. Soon my whole legs are numb, then my arms feel like they're going to sleep. But I manage to sit down on a bench in front of a beer garden first, to try to digest what's happened.

Then I remember, struggle up. No, no. I must hurry. I run like an invalid many city blocks to my bank, clear out all my savings. Do I have enough?

The boys will need food. Vati needs a lawyer.

Who's going to pay for everything?

❦ ❦ ❦

Julie's funeral.

So many people come to see the glamorous yet tragic *Frau Doktor* put to rest.

So jung, so jung. So *schoen*. Her age is one hot topic. She was only 45.

Another is her many children. How did that poor woman manage to raise such a large brood? She was a saint, a pure saint.

I hear those comments. It's background noise. It doesn't mean anything. Yes, Julie died young. And yes, she had 11 kids, the smaller ones of which are now orphans for however long Vati is locked up in jail....

But that's not the tragedy at hand. That tragedy is

that Julie's funeral has been delayed for so many weeks. Immediately after her death, her body was gutted by the medical examiner. Every one of her organs was removed. Cut open, sliced, diced, put under the microscope. Examined many times. Dunked into chemicals, observed for reactions....

Some of Julie's vital parts are still in the coroner's glass jars. Or squeezed between thin glass slides. Or in vials, tubes, stored in refrigerators....

I don't know how much of her is actually in the closed casket that sits on a scaffold by the open grave. I do know that Vati is still in jail. He continues to be in investigative custody. I go to see him once. Not of my own free will, however. I'm summoned to the downtown Munich Police Precinct. Walk into an ancient building with worn stairs. Luckily my legs have returned to normal. I take an oath in front of a jovial magistrate to tell the truth.

What is the truth?

I'll do it, I vow, my heart heavy. For once I'll tell everything I know. Another man, this one in uniform, stretches behind a desk. Asks me to sit down, get comfortable, then dives in: What unusual sexual practices did the detained man carry out?

I blink, blink, to get over the embarrassment I feel, when another policeman barges in and snaps: Idiot. That's one of his girls.

I know, that's why—

No, I mean one of his *daughters*, not his girl-friends—

Oh, well.

From then on it's just chitchat. Before I'm released, I'm allowed to see Vati. A guard brings him to a room that's divided in two parts, one for the visitors, and the other one, separated by chicken wire, for the prisoners.

Vati comes in looking short. No shoes. He's walking funny with just his socks on. They need darning. I wish I'd brought yarn and needle. I look at him through the wire. He's as embarrassed as I was over that sex question. I don't know what to say, except, *Wie geht's?*

And what else can he say, except *Gut*? Then there's little else to say besides talking about what food they serve him and when he thinks he's going to get out. *Bald, bald, jaja,* he says looking like a lion that has been defanged.

How soon? I persist. I've put my whole life on hold. Not that that's anything new. I've done it for so many years—for two decades. So, again I'm consumed with family obligations. Karli is the main one. He rarely asks about his mother because I make sure he has little free time. I'm constantly taking him for a walk, to play in the park, to go to the market, buy him anything he wants to eat. I can't afford to buy him any books. But I tell him stories I make up about brave little boys and girls who never cry and are shipwrecked and have many exciting adventures. Live happily ever after in America.

People often compliment me on my cute little "son." At first I correct them. Tell him he's my baby brother. Then I don't bother anymore to set them straight. Let them go ahead, judge me, let them think I had a baby at 15. I can read their thoughts: Poor dumb gal, got herself pregnant so young, now look at her, teehee....

But what do I care about what people think? If they think their stares and snide comments make me feel ashamed, they don't know what shame is. Besides, I wish they were right. Raising an illegitimate child as a young, broke single mom would be a snap compared to what I have to do.

One day Karli does ask: Where is Mummy?

In heaven, I say, just like my Mutti. I was about your age when she went away.

Why?

I don't know.

But that isn't the kind of thing to tell Vati who is caged behind the chicken wire wall in the Munich City jail. I want to scream at him: Did you do it? Kill her. Did—you—do—it?

But what if he says yes? Then the guard watching us might pass Vati's confession along to the authorities. Which will mean I'll have to be Karli's keeper forever.

And if Vati says no, then I won't know any more than I do now. Which is, either he did it or he didn't. It changes nothing. For if he didn't kill Julie, he panicked, lost his head over nothing which makes him a total fool. Or he panicked over something he's done previously and never owned up to—maybe some other crime or crimes....

And if he did murder her and that's the reason he panicked, then I'm the daughter of a killer. That's not something I want to be, since I'm already a German, which is disgrace enough in the eyes of the world, the universe. I am the offspring of a killer nation. With a shudder, I think of Karli's future. Won't it tear him apart when he finds out that his father killed his mother?

If it's true, that is. But what is *true*? I don't know anymore. I have never known. I have lived in a Bavaria that, from the outside, now that the last traces of war have been painted over, looks to be as close to heaven as any part of the world can be. The picturesque villages, the thriving cities with palaces of glass and expensive stone, the crystal-blue lakes, pristine meadows....The majestic Alps reaching for the sky....

And yet—what kind of people live in these villages? In the beautiful bustling cities? Dear hardworking farmers? Smart townspeople studiously pursuing their work? Able artisans and artists? Brilliant thinkers like Vati?

Or cold-hearted killers? Brutal butchers?

Or both?

Oh, what mountains of human ashes were washed into the beautiful lakes and have settled on their bottoms? What wildflower meadows have been fertilized with the remains of millions of innocent people?

Are the Alps the earth's granite praying hands, Dürer's hands, asking God for forgiveness?

I don't know, and I can find out nothing new the day I visit Vati in jail. Only five minutes have passed. Still a lot of time left of the visiting hour, but I'm tongue-tied. Have nothing to say. Of course there's the weather to discuss. The *Foehn*. The warm wind that blows from the Alps that gives many people headaches.

Lucky people. What luxury to have a nice little

headache caused by some force of nature and not from the relentless hitting my head on invisible walls....

But I have to keep talking, to distract Vati, entertain him. When I run out of small talk, I attack the guard verbally.

He's calling Vati "Vierling," as if he were a common man. A laborer, ditch digger, nothing but dirt. "Thirty more minutes, Vierling."

How dare you talk to my father like that? I yell at the guard. Don't you know who he is?

Who is he? I ask myself at the same time while the guard grins maliciously. Sure do, he says. *Richtig interessant.* Mighty interesting, Miss, to have *him* drop in on our little jailhouse here, huh-huh-huh. New developments every day since he got here....

Vati looks even more embarrassed. I wish I had kept my mouth shut.

When it's time for me to leave, Vati wants to shake hands, but there's no opening in the chicken wire big enough for him to stick his handsome hand through. And pressing his palm against the wire still keeps him from making physical contact with me. The only solution is to reach over the high wire meshing. I'm wearing high heels, so it's nothing for me to stretch my arm way up. But without shoes, Vati can't reach the top. No matter how far he stretches the tips of his fingers to touch mine over the mesh, he can't do it. He's shrunk, so he has to jump.

First he hops, hops, hops. Each time he almost makes it, but he still can't quite touch my fingertips. The guard cackles at Vati's pitiful tries. Hop-hop.

Vati steps back. Before the guard can stop him he

takes a running start, speeds up and flings himself at the chicken wire. By sheer will power he digs in a toe, just for a split second, and soars up. Is in the air, suspended, a young man again, color in his handsome face, great muscle tone, a human masterpiece, like during his best days. He smacks my fingertips with his whole hand.

The chicken wire wall trembles even after Vati lands back on the floor on his side of the room. Bread and water for you for three days, Vierling, the furious guard decrees, clangs keys, chains, and metal rings. That was against regulations.

Vati laughs. I know why. Bread and water is a feast in our family.

As Vati is led off in shackles, he says, I'll be out soon.

Sure, I say, *sure. Wiedersehn.* But I'm not sure at all. Every day the newspapers keep quoting a detective who announces: There's more involved in the Dr. Vierling Case than meets the eye. More, much more....

Right. What's involved are 11 kids. Eleven young lives. Some of the brothers are too young to make it on their own. So the older of the little boys have been farmed out to various distant family members. Or been shipped off to farms that need cheap labor. Despite their starvation childhood, the little brothers are all growing up into strong and stocky boys. That makes them prime candidates for free child labor—little farmhands who can be overworked day and night because they have no other place to go to.

Orphans—that's what they are. We all are, one way or another.

This is Hitler's legacy—a generation of orphans.

And that's exactly what we look like at Julie's funeral—a bunch of lost, abandoned straggly kids. Street urchins, fugitives, vagabonds.

The cemetery is on Munich's outskirts—a nice well-kept *Friedhof*. The grave sites are manicured. Many are miniature flower gardens. Others are mausoleums the size of small homes. But to one side is still just a field, and now a hole gapes there.

Later a raw-looking jagged rock will become Julie's headstone. Her name will be engraved on this rock. And a sturdy live fir tree will be her main floral ornament and outgrow the rock, make the grave look just like a part of nature again.

But for now Julie's open grave is a wound in the soil. Her black casket awaits the blessings of two priests. Incense will swirl with long Latin lamentations. Holy wisps and words will rise to heaven. The coffin will be lowered into the hole in the ground.

A huge crowd in mourning has gathered. Many people from Starnberg, Diessen, and Munich have arrived in black limousines. Close and distant relatives, neighbors and friends from Traunstein, Weiden, Ruesselsheim and Cologne have come. Some even from East Germany. The Berlin Wall isn't up yet. Plus, scads of curiosity seekers have formed a solid ring around the funeral site. It's a fashion show of black lace, black hats, black suits, coats, capes. And sounds of muffled crying and suppressed sobs are background music while the ring of onlookers keeps growing.

In the middle of it we kids huddle. Everyone is

here, all 11 of us. Some of us have traveled great distances. We wear whatever we have, brown, blue, green, red, yellow outfits that look ragged. Except for Heda, we wear patched sweaters, pinned-together skirts, ill-fitting shirts, outgrown pants, jackets that have been passed down too many times. We have on scuffed shoes, with their heels ground down, floppy sandals, knee socks with the elastic gone. And not one of us has a handkerchief to wipe off the streaks of dirt I didn't catch earlier on Karli.

No matter how I tried to fix up my siblings, we look like we always do, like a motley bunch of kids picked up from across the country. Better washed this time, sure, and hair combed, but rag-tag nonetheless. Our hair colors range from a brown that's almost black to white-blond. Same goes for our eye colors. They go from light gray-blue to vivid blue, to light green-brown to stark and piercing brown that's almost black.

Our complexion? That too ranges from white-white to the darkest of tans.

We're here at our mother/step mother's funeral. Our father/step father's in jail accused of killing her, and we know it's probably the last time we'll ever be together again, all of us.

And yet there's not one tear on any of our faces. We're all dry-eyed.

We look grim, which is normal for us. Rare is the ability among us to smile anyway. And there's nothing to smile about today. We're shocked, upset, but also feel strangely vindicated. The older ones of us say with their eyes what we all always expected: Didn't we always know it would end up badly?

What other ending, except the death of one of them, could there have been? Just another death in a land steeped in death.

But did that death have to be this tragic? This mysterious?

Why couldn't it have been cut and dried?

And why are we here, except to please the curious crowd? We know there's no Julie in the casket. Julie is the blonde tall belle from Cologne. The young woman with luxurious, wheat-colored coils of hair she wears like a crown. With that perfect peach skin, those sparkling blue eyes, and talents so enormous she could've run the grandest estate in the land, could've single-handedly ruled over a major dukedom.

She was royalty.

I remember when she first married Vati, what a whirlwind she was. So full of such hope, so much energy. Such style and flair—

Now her liver is sliced to pieces. Her stomach contents are still preserved somewhere. Her brain has been removed from her skull and been cut apart. Her dear, brave heart that fought with all its might against dirt, destruction, and despair every day has been dissected.

Damn me. *Why couldn't I be the daughter she needed?*

And why couldn't I keep my own Mutti alive, and not let those damn blood clots suck the life out of her like leeches?

I feel my face burning like it's made of hot stone. But I will not cry. Too late for tears anyway. Time to cry was back then, not now. Barbara's long been

eaten by worms, and in the casket that's being lowered in front of us, there's only bits and pieces of
Julie. But I can't get her face out of my mind, when
she showed me the frog. Or the vision of her ancient
elegant suit that's now covering the holes cut into
her. Oh, her long legs, her slim feet wearing her finest
black shoes....Or maybe the coroner just dumped
whatever was left of her into the coffin. Just some
chunks of her, odds and ends, arms and legs, bones....

That my siblings are thinking along the same lines
is evident by the small sounds of hurt that erupt
from them. There's an uncomfortable shifting in the
bunch around me. An uneasy fidgeting of kids that
want to get away from all this. Get away and be carefree kids once in our lives. But of course we can't.
The hundreds of mourners hold us enclosed. They
have come to see 11 kids cry. Can't wait to see at
least the girls dissolve in tears.

We don't. We're too bitter about what happened.
Too destroyed. Our father and our mother survived
the war only to be wiped out in its aftermath. I
remember Shakespeare from school: *The evil that
men do lives after them....*

Is this the punishment for Vati, because he kept
his eyes shut to the killing ovens when he should've
kept them open?

But why is it us kids who're crushed?

The priests finish their rites. The coffin has dis-
appeared. Oh, relief. We kids will make it out of the
cemetery dry-eyed. Now only a few more words,
some litany or other. Nuns are like black statues. A
whole contingent has come from the hospital Julie

spent so much time in. This is the first I've been able to distinguish the nuns from the many other mourners. Their rosaries are white pearls gliding through their fingers while they murmur, turn to leave.

The funeral is over, yet none of us kids have broken down.

Then crack! A loud noise silences the nuns and the rest of the crowd. The loud noise comes from Hansi, the oldest boy in the family. The most stoic of all my eight brothers. The noise wrenches from deep inside his chest. It's a sound that's inhuman. Such a pure sound of agony, of bones cracking, metal bursting. No, of a heart splitting, of a soul crying out. But magnified a hundred thousand times.

Dead silence after that sound. Then the murmuring of the nuns again, more tears flow among the spectators. Some small outcries echo, more sobs come, this time they babble freely, like a brook.

Still none of us kids cry. Hansi's face remains unchanged too. It would be superficial to boo-hoo. We just huddle close together in our refugee outfits. Pat each other in silence. We know more than ever who we are: We're Germans after the Holocaust.

❧ ❧ ❧

On the way out of the cemetery, I stumble behind a group of well-dressed women who're in a hushed but excited exchange of information.

One of them says: Really too bad, too bad....He killed another one.

I freeze on the gravel walkway, and the women turn, recognize in my face traces of Vati's noble bone structure. They notice the ragged clothes I have on

and my stony expression, and scurry off like cock-
roaches when the light comes on.

🍎 🍎 🍎

I ask Heda about what I overheard: What were
those women talking about?

She's about to climb into a gleaming dark-blue
Mercedes, go back to her house in the fashionable
suburbs. It's over with, done. That embarrassing
funeral is behind her. Maybe she can go on vacation
to Mallorca or Majorca—anywhere, until whatever
scandal is left to deal with is over with, OK? All this
disgrace, this vulgar gossiping. She doesn't deserve
it and is in a rush to get away.

I grab her sleeve. Just tell me, Heda.

I guess those women think Vati did it.

No. I mean about that expression they used.
"Another one?"

Heda waves the car on, walks toward an over-
hanging beech tree with me, stops. I don't want to
tell you.

Why?

Because it'll hurt you and you don't need anymore....She falls silent.

Right, but tell me anyway. Please, please.

She hesitates. I guess, they meant Aunt Erna.

Vati's beloved younger sister?

Yes.

What happened?

Heda's silent again, seems to be fighting with herself. *Ach.*

Go on, I say urgently. I asked one of the brothers

to look after Karli, but he has to catch a bus shortly. So time is short. Since I remember hearing about Tante Erna before, I try to help Heda reveal what she knows by asking: Wasn't Erna the one who married that dwarf?

Midget.

Yes, a tiny man with a hunchback.

That's right, Eri. Vati used to talk about her all the time years ago.

I remember it.

But what he didn't talk about was that everybody really worried about Tante Erna. That she either wouldn't get pregnant or maybe she would and have a little midget.

A baby hunchback midget?

Yes. So anyway, Eri. Vati gave her some kind of medicine. To help her either not have a baby—

Or have a healthy one. So what?

This was during the war and Vati was pretty much tied down. He couldn't travel like he wanted to, nobody could. Anyway, next thing Erna's pregnant. And by the time Vati gets some furlough, he finds her at the hospital.

Did Erna have the baby?

Yes. Vati was sent down to the hospital's laundry room. And there was Erna lying naked on the wash table, with the baby. Both dead as doornails.

Oh no, she was his favorite sister, wasn't she?

Yes, yes. Bye now.

No, Heda, wait. I grab her, make her stay. Stop lying.

It's all true. It's not just a rumor.

I don't mean that. I'm sure it's true. It's too grue-some otherwise. But that's not what those women were talking about.

Heda folds her arms. Suit yourself. That's all I know.

Uh-uh. You know more, you always do.

No, I don't.

Then what did you mean about hurting me? Huh? I didn't even know Tante Erna. So that's not it. There's something else. Out with it.

Heda shakes her head. *Nein, nein.*

Then you keep Karli, OK? He's all yours. I'll drop him off at your house. I'll show up at your next sym-phony meeting, all right? With a mop and bucket and hair tied up in a rag and let everybody know I'm your sister.

Heda flinches. Don't. She puts an arm around me: Do you know that you could've been *somebody*? That's why I'm not telling you.

Been somebody?

Yes, you were smart. Real smart when you were a child. You had rickets and Mutti had to carry you everywhere. She fussed over you, nursed you, paid attention to you. Remember that story you wrote in second grade? The nuns read it to every grade level, mine too.

You never told me.

I was envious, because you were so smart back then. Now look at you. You're nothing but a maid. A cleaning woman. A factory worker. Just look at your hands.

We compare hands and mine are hard, calloused and ancient next to hers.

It's not over yet. I can still go to college...some day....

But don't you see? It *is* too late for you. Your grades are no good. You know nothing. You never read a book. You have no culture, no manners, nothing. You're always rushing off to another hard job.

Who has time to read?

That's what I mean. All these years of being Julie's slave. You could never concentrate on your school work, so you got dumb. Your talent got wasted. You got stepped on, squashed. Now you'll never be what you could've been. It's too late, too late. But if Mutti had lived....Heda looks at her watch. Just remember I didn't want to tell you, you made me.

So?

Ach, ach, ach. Vati. You know how he is.

He didn't turn me into a slave.

No, but he caused it.

What did he do?

Mutti's health wasn't good. You know, having so many kids in such a short time can deplete anyone. Look at what it did to poor Julie. So Mutti had circular hair loss. Maybe it was her nerves. Or from worrying about Vati and his girlfriends, I don't know. I only know she loved him....

And? My heart is pounding. And?

So he gave her something and she took it without questioning him. Swallowed it, every time he gave it to her.

What was it?

Hormones.

And? And?

Hormones have side effects, Eri.
What kind of side effects? I'm whispering now.
They cause blood clots.

CHAPTER 17

Tomorrows

Must get away from Germany or drown. Or die some other way. So that becomes my goal from then on—how to escape. Now. When my soldier returns from the alert relaxed and carefree and again brings up the topic of us getting married, I ask:

When?

His green eyes spark: Whenever you say so, he says.

Next time I see him, he hands me pounds of crisp sheets. Here you go. I'm told it takes forever to do the preliminary paperwork.

I can believe it, I say, flipping through the fresh pile of sheets that are etched with hundreds of questions in fine print. All deal with me, my background and family:

List your parents and siblings, their birth dates, clubs, memberships. Where we lived year after year starting with birth. Give references and names of neighbors. Include addresses of family doctor, dentist, teachers, principal....

Plus several physicals are required and a session with the chaplain for pre-marriage counseling. Also an interview with the soldier's commanding officer.

While marriage between the GIs and their foreign gals isn't *verboten*, it's frowned upon, especially by the pretty American secretaries who, lipsticked and noses powdered, preside over the realms of rules, regulations and appointment books.

So filling out all those forms with their tiny lines in quadruplicate seems an impossibility. But I stay up one night, print something in every single space. Not enough room for all my brothers and sisters' names, of course. I have to relegate some of them to the spaces left for neighbors, friends, classmates....

The army chaplain, however, turns out to be nice. Talks about the biggest glitch in the marriages of young soldiers. That's for the new wife to have a separate bank account. Don't do it, he says.

I have the equivalent of two bucks in my purse, thus can promise with all my heart I'm not even thinking about a separate account.

The commanding officer is nice too. Says: Give up Catholicism and join the Baptist Church to which my soldier belongs. Would you?

I'll do it at once, I say. Done.

Already the waiting period for our forthcoming marriage has been cut by half a year. No counseling needed, since I'm no longer Catholic and too poor to have a bank account.

Now on to the physicals, with all the various

tests, starting with urine, blood, TB, lots of other checks to rule out venereal diseases. And some fees to be paid.

I manage to get an appointment in days rather than six months. And when the male receptionist at the Second Field Hospital calls me up to his desk out of the sea of other waiting potential war brides, he blinks. Looks at me hard. Can see beneath the mask I wear. Can see all I've been through already. Can read the signs of urgency on me.

I'm despair personified.

So without any tests at all, he goes stamp, stamp, stamp.

Turns papers, flips through reams of sheets, flings carbon copies left and right, and again and again pounds a blue seal onto many pages. Stamp. Stamp. Stamp.

Pockets the fees and one more time: Stamp. Not on my forehead, but it feels like it.

All done.

What should have stretched out 12 months or longer—the preliminary application, the filing for immigration, the permission to get married to a U.S. citizen, and all the various interviews, meetings, check-ups—is over with in a few nail-biting days.

🍒 🍒 🍒

But it isn't all over. Germany wants a little cash too.

I submit copies of the myriads of stamped forms, more fees. Then there's the civil ceremony at the Munich *Standesamt I* to go through. It's attended by several of my brothers, wearing what they wore to the funeral.

At the time Vati is still being held in "investigative custody." So we rush through the rites. Afterwards my soldier and I take off on a three-day honeymoon to Berchtesgaden, where the U.S. Army has established a vacation retreat for the military.

It's near the site of Hitler's Alpine chalet, formerly known as Eagle's Nest. A long tunnel, carved into the mountain, leads to an elevator rising to the chalet. We amble through the picturesque village, go sightseeing at the Eagle's Nest.

My husband is elated. He now has someone who admires him, hangs on his every word non-stop. What a diversion between all those fun alerts, another of which is coming up shortly.

But I'm tense. So tense. What if this is all a dream? What if I wake up tomorrow and I'm back on my raw, skinny knees having to scrub those huge piles of dirty laundry again with no soap and ice-cold water while my stomach is rumbling from hunger?

What if the American secretaries have gone over my papers with a fine-tooth comb by now and found the mistakes?

What if hands reach out from the graves of the six million, yank me back, their owners hissing: Hey, you there, German girl. You're not getting away that easy from the killing fields....

But finally, finally it's time.

Birds migrate; I emigrate.

🐞 🐞 🐞

At the Munich Hauptbahnhof, mid-June, 1961.

I'm so happy. It's only half an hour till the train

leaves. First I'll go to Frankfurt am Main. That's near Ruesselsheim, where I lied to all those angry orchard owners and gardeners, whose crops my brothers stole. Where I almost lost Julie's money in the tunnel.

But now I can smile about my life because I am *this* close to salvation. From Frankfurt a silver plane will spirit me to New York, to safety, freedom, a better life.

My true life.

I'm replicating my Mutti's escape away from East Germany. West—I'm heading west just as far away from my past as I can. Away from the war, from all that pain.

Twenty more minutes. My rescue train looks huge. I board it early, eagerly. It's like a moving fortress, all black steel and powerful. None of my brothers and sisters have come to see me off, even though I told everyone what time the train is leaving.

Heda's excuse: The New Theater's fund-raiser is tonight. She has to prepare for the event, get a facial, manicure, new hairdo, go to the safe, get her good jewels out. Those things take time, Eri.

I understand. I'm just a younger sibling who's amounted to nothing. Just another family disappointment, but so what? Now I'm emigrating. Actually I'm fleeing.

Hansi can't come either. He's forging ahead with his dream of becoming a top representative for an international company. IBM. That means he has to travel a lot; he speaks French almost as well as German and is on the go constantly.

Heini really can't come to the station. He's in

Australia, starting a brand-new life. Two of the younger brothers will join him later.

And Ger? She's still the darling of the art school in Augsburg. Her talent to bring beauty to a plain sheet of paper with nothing but a few sure strokes of her pencil or a piece of charcoal continues to grow. Her inner and outer grace shield her from reality. It's as if she's painted herself a peaceful past, a lovely present, and a golden future with her oil paints.

On this day, her younger sister is leaving the country forever. She's going to America, yet Ger concludes her last phone call to me with: *Ciao*. See you soon....

And Rudi? He's striking out on his own too. He's bound for Greece and later India. Ever since the day the government announced: A new German army is in the making. All males born in 1939 and later must henceforth register with....

That includes him. So he makes hurried plans to leave the country. Not again, he says and packs a bag. I agree: *Nie wieder!*

The other brothers are too young or too far away to come see me off. I didn't expect them to anyway. Fleeing is best done alone, without an audience.

Now I'm in the massive train. My small bag has been stored in the overhead luggage compartment. It's a nice sunny day—perfect. Five more minutes until departure time. Please, let nothing go wrong. I wish I could make the clock speed up. Go, time, go.

Looking out the window, I'm nervous. What if there's a delay? What if—? What if...? Through the crowds milling on the platform, I see an unusual movement. It's as if the people shift to make room for something—someone. Vati.

He comes running along the train looking for me. I shrink away from the window, but a whistle reassures me. I'm all right. The train's getting ready to pull out. Vati has spotted me, runs faster to catch up with me. Does so and smiles. He stands under the open train window and throws me a kiss. *Verzeihung, bitte!* he shouts. His eyes fill with tears.

Forgive me please? For what? I wonder.

For what he did or didn't do to Julie?

For what he did or didn't do to my Mutti?

For what he did or didn't do to me?

For what he didn't do to help the Jews! He never took responsibility for not doing anything to help them. Never said he was sorry.

Before I can ask him any of the myriad of questions I have, before I can vent my anger, the train starts to pull out. Vati has to step back, but not before he thrusts a bouquet of flowers at me. It's wrapped in green tissue papers. So it wasn't stolen. He actually bought these flowers. And I know he has no money. His cheeks are sunk in, his white hair has thinned, his muscular body shriveled. He's a bent gnarled tree on the Zugspitze. His spine is broken. Now without the mantle of flesh it's obvious. The irises of his mesmerizing eyes are a washed-out slate color —pale, powerless. His old eyes fill with tears.

I don't want his flowers, no way. I refuse to take them, but the train starts to move and Vati starts running alongside of it, still holding the bouquet. Shoves it high at me. Please, take it, his eyes beg, please.

Tears stream down his face leaving trails. Snail trails.

The train speeds up. Vati has to struggle to keep up with it. I can't stand what it does to him. He's having to push himself so. He has to gasp for breath. So I reach out, grab the stupid bouquet. Waste of money! He'll need every penny he can get from now on. Doesn't he know that? Since his release from jail on the grounds of "insufficient evidence," he's been faced with all those bills that the sale of Julie's house didn't cover. He's also having to find a home for Karli. Has to look after the other boys too. So why does he waste cash on this trash?

I plan to toss the flowers out once we're around the first bend. I want nothing from that man, nothing. He's a stranger to me, worse than a stranger. He's an enemy. He has hurt me. The wounds run deep. I never want to see him again (and only do once more, years later).

Vati took my *Heimat*, my homeland, away from me. My language, my heart, my pride, my me. What might I have been had Mutti lived?

He recedes into the distance. He's stopped running and is waving wildly with a smile. His teeth are still the whitest I've ever seen. A skeleton's white teeth, a grinning mask of death....

We chug around a curve and Vati's erased. I let out my breath. I have done it, wiped out the past. Wiped out the shame, the heartache. It's over for me. I exhale slowly, again and congratulate myself on having gotten this far.

I peel back the green tissue paper shrouding the bouquet to get a look at the flowers before pitching them out the window. The paper is folded to perfection. A pretty pink velvet ribbon decorates it at the bottom. A piece of tape closes the top. Must have cost a damn bundle.

I rip into it. Before I get the paper all the way open, a lovely aroma hits me. It's as if those flowers are trying their best to please me and have concentrated all their good smells into one powerful waft of sweet perfume.

I yank the paper open all the way.

White roses!

The train gathers speed. I bury my face in the flowers. I'm on the first leg of my journey to America.

I am going to fly across the ocean. To a new life. If only Mutti could see me.